This is a fascinating historical [...] for preachers. It stimulated me [...] relationship of word and Spirit. Whether you end up agreeing with the author or not, I commend it to anyone who wants to think seriously about what is going on when scripture is opened up in the pulpit, and what the Reformers really said about this.

LEE GATISS,
Director of Church Society
Adjunct Lecturer at Wales Evangelical School of Theology, Bridgend, Wales

This is a book that all who preach and teach God's word should read. Being confident that the Spirit of God is at work when the Word of God is taught will make us work hard in our preparation and will make us more dependent on God in our prayers.

JUSTIN MOTE,
Director of the North West Ministry Training Course
and Associate Minister, St Andrew's Church, Leyland, Lancashire

Preaching with Spiritual Power is the first book-length treatment of an important issue that has been simmering just under the surface British Evangelicalism for a number of years. Ralph Cunnington (wisely) restricts himself to only one area of the debate--historical theology. While these pages will not close discussion of Calvin's teaching, or of the larger issues on which they touch, I hope they will not lead to a full-blown controversy, but to a closer examination of the Scriptures.

SINCLAIR B. FERGUSON,
Associate Preacher, St Peter's Free Church, Dundee

As one who shares some of the general concerns of Cunningham's interlocutors regarding a growing intellectualism in expository preaching and a concomitant lack of emphasis on the outpouring of the Spirit as the great need of the contemporary church, I nevertheless found the argument of this volume both timely and persuasive.

Is it possible that the Word of God may be faithfully preached and yet remain void of the presence of the Spirit of God? Carefully examining Calvin's sacramental thought, Cunningham's answer highlights the vital Christological concept of "distinction without separation" as the missing category in much of the contemporary debate. When the Word is truly expounded the Spirit is always present, though not always to bless. Like the two natures of Christ, or the sacramental sign and thing signified, Word and Spirit, for Calvin, are inseparable but not indistinguishable: there is a union but not an identity between them. While there remains vital work to be done in addressing important differences between the older and the newer reformed evangelicals on the issue of preaching and the work of the Holy Spirit, Ralph Cunningham has made a valuable contribution to the debate. More than that, however, it is an encouraging reminder that God himself attends the Word in the presence of the Spirit, and in this confidence his ministers may speak and labor with holy boldness.

DAVID STRAIN,
Senior Minister, First Presbyterian Church, Jackson, Mississippi

One does not have to agree with every jot and tittle of Ralph's argument to find this book stimulating, challenging and timely. It is of great importance that our doctrine of preaching is robust and biblical and I found this volume's careful assessment of Calvin a great help in achieving these aims.

ADRIAN REYNOLDS,
Director of Ministry, The Proclamation Trust and
Associate Minister, East London Tabernacle, London

The relationship between Word and Spirit is a matter of crucial importance. Ralph Cunnington provides a most careful analysis in some depth of the historical data concerning Lutheran and Reformed views of the subject and thereby takes the debate forwards in a very helpful manner.

ROBERT STRIVENS,
Principal, London Theological Seminary, London

Although he is dealing with a complex and controversial subject, Ralph Cunnington brings to this helpful study a clear mind, scholarly thoroughness and deep pastoral concern. He sets Calvin's views of Word and Spirit in the wider context of the views of other influential Reformers such as Luther, Zwingli and Bullinger, and allows the evidence to speak for itself. Making important connections with Calvin's sacramental theology, he argues convincingly that Calvin held Word and Spirit firmly together, such that when the Word is received by faith, it will be a source of blessing to believers. The implications for our understanding of Calvin and also for our practice of preaching are significant.

DAVID MCKAY,
Professor of Systematic Theology, Ethics and Apologetics,
Reformed Theological College, Belfast,
Minister of Shaftesbury Square Reformed Presbyterian Church, Belfast

Evangelicals are sadly disagreed about the relationship between the Word and the Spirit in preaching. Some argue that it cannot be presumed that the preaching of the Word will be accompanied by the presence and power of the Spirit, and they assert that to believe otherwise will inevitably lead preachers to place confidence in their exegetical skill and presentational techniques, rather than on the necessity of urgent prayer. They claim that their critique of contemporary preaching is supported by the teaching of John Calvin. In this careful study in historical theology Ralph Cunnington shows that Calvin gives no support the idea that the Spirit's accompaniment of the preaching of the Word will be sporadic or unpredictable. Drawing on Calvin's wider theology of the sacraments, he maintains that the Word and the Spirit are distinct but inseparable. Far from producing self-reliance, this conviction will motivate preachers to be prayerfully dependent upon God and rightly diligent in their preparation. This short, readable and relevant book will be a great help to preachers, equipping them to navigate these contemporary controversies and providing them with a proper theological understanding of their vital work. More importantly will bring them reassurance that the Spirit will always accompany the Word they proclaim, whether to bring judgement or blessing to their hearers.

JOHN STEVENS,
National Director,
Fellowship of Independent Evangelical Churches (FIEC)

PREACHING WITH SPIRITUAL POWER

Calvin's Understanding
of Word and Spirit in Preaching

Ralph Cunnington

MENTOR

Ralph Cunnington is Pastor of City Church Manchester. After seven years working as a university law lecturer he trained for pastoral ministry at Wales Evangelical School of Theology (WEST) and Westminster Seminary London and was then Assistant Pastor at Aigburth Community Church, Liverpool. Ralph is a member of the FIEC and Affinity Theological teams and is editor of Foundations.

Copyright © Ralph Cunnington 2015

paperback ISBN 978-1-78191-601-8
epub ISBN 978-1-78191-654-4
mobi ISBN 978-1-78191-655-1

Published in 2015
in the
Mentor Imprint
by
Christian Focus Publications Ltd.,
Geanies House, Fearn, Ross-shire,
IV20 1TW, Scotland, Great Britain.
www.christianfocus.com

Cover design by Daniel Van Straaten

Printed by
Bell and Bain, Glasgow

MIX
Paper from
responsible sources
FSC® C007785

CONTENTS

FOREWORD

In this book Ralph Cunnington presents a careful evaluation of John Calvin's theology of preaching. It is well known that Calvin held that the Word and the Holy Spirit are inseparably related. This conviction has subsequently been a hallmark of the Reformed churches. The Westminster Assembly (1643–47), in its *Confession of Faith,* spelled this out repeatedly in connection with revelation, calling, the ministry, sanctification, good works and so on.

The author makes a clear connection between Calvin's pronouncements on preaching and his doctrine of the sacraments. He builds on the work of Brian Gerrish. Writing on Calvin's treatment of the Lord's Supper, Gerrish distinguished between symbolic memorialism, the idea that the sacrament was purely symbolic (associated with Huldrych Zwingli); symbolic parallelism, the claim that God's grace operated in tandem with our participation but was not directly brought about or caused by it (Heinrich Bullinger); and symbolic instrumentalism, which he maintained Calvin taught, in which Christ effects his gracious work in and by the sacraments. Cunnington argues persuasively that this was true of Calvin's discussion of preaching as well.

It is not hard to see the reasons that underlie such an inseparable connection. The trinity is three distinct hypostases but one
indivisible being. Neither the Father, nor the Son, nor the Holy
Spirit are for one instant divisible or separable from the others.
For Calvin, as for the tradition stretching back to the Cappado-
cians of the fourth century and Augustine of the fifth, the Word
and the Spirit were distinct but indivisible.

Calvin had to distance himself from two alternative poles. On
the one hand there was the idea that the Word itself had power
of itself, that the working of the Spirit was to be identified with
the Word. This is sometimes attributed to Luther and Lutherans,
but debatably so. On the other hand, there were the Anabaptists
and others who maintained that the Spirit could and did work
independently of the Word, whether written or preached. Such
a view opens up the prospect of fresh revelations from the Spirit
unconnected with Scripture.

This debate is also a current one. Some have argued that the
Spirit works automatically through the Word preached. If this is
so, all the preacher needs to do is to explain the meaning of the
Bible. From this, the distinctiveness of preaching in the Biblical
sense, as a herald appealing to the consciences of the hearers
appears to be blunted. Philip Eveson has argued that this is a
characteristic of the theology of Moore College, at the heart of
the conservative Anglican diocese of Sydney; he suggests that it
has been widely influential. Others have contended that this is
a Lutheran emphasis and a major threat to the life and spiritual
vitality of the church.

On the other hand, many of those influenced by the Welsh
revivalist tradition, in countering what they perceive to be the
shortcomings of what they term 'Moore theology', consider that
the Spirit cannot be trapped by the Word but is free to work
independently; moreover, he often leaves the preached Word
effectively powerless. So as a consequence it is up to the church
to pray, to storm the gates of heaven so as to persuade God to act.

How does Calvin fit into this scenario? What has he to teach us? Are his views still of relevance and help today? In answer to these questions Ralph Cunnington is an excellent guide. With careful and incisive scholarship, and writing that is both clear and cogent, he steers a sure and reliable course between these two poles. He recognizes that advocates of both positions are deeply concerned for the same goals as he is, for the effective proclamation of the gospel, the powerful work of the Holy Spirit in our own times. In this spirit, as a co-belligerent and a friendly colleague, he calls us back to Calvin, as a major source behind the classic Reformed confessions. Here we find rich wisdom and secure help; I am convinced this will buttress and empower all who preach the gospel in times as potentially troubled as those of Calvin.

Robert Letham
Wales Evangelical School of Theology

ACKNOWLEDGMENTS

This is a book on preaching borne out of a love for God's Word and a love for those whom I have had the privilege to pastor at City Church Manchester and Aigburth Community Church, Liverpool. Thank you to the members of both churches for your love, support and encouragement, and for making Hebrews 13:17 a reality in my life. Thanks are also due to my colleagues at both churches, especially Steve Palframan and Matt Waldock, for enabling me to have the time and space to write this book. Much of the research that forms the basis of this book was undertaken in the libraries of the Wales Evangelical School of Theology and London Theological Seminary. Thanks are due to the staff at both institutions as well as at Westminster Theological Seminary Philadelphia. I am especially grateful to Dr Robert Letham who has acted as an academic mentor to me on various projects over the past five years. I am privileged to benefit from your wisdom and direction.

The debate with which this book seeks to engage is an intra-mural one, taking place within the confines not just of evangelicalism but of Reformed theology. Sometimes it is necessary to contend for the truth in the heat of a battle for orthodoxy over core gospel doctrines. Thankfully this is not such a situation and I have benefited enormously from interacting with Robert Strivens, Stuart Olyott, Philip Eveson, Hywel Jones and Eryl Davies at various stages of the writing of this book. These men are older, wiser and more experienced than me and I am enormously grateful to them for the time they have given to engaging with my work and improving it. I am also indebted to Philip Ross and Emma Cunnington for their comments on and editing of earlier versions of this manuscript.

My wonderful wife, Anna, has been a constant support during the writing of this book. As I said on our wedding day, I love your inner beauty which, far from fading, has grown each year of our marriage. Thank you also to my children, Sophie, Zach and Jacob for putting up with Daddy's busyness; my prayer is that you will come to the Word with faith and know the Spirit accompanying it for your blessing.

Soli Deo gloria can sound trite but it should not. This book is about the power of God and it is written by one of many millions who knows and has experienced that power. Eighteen years ago I opened the Spirit-inspired Word and read it with new eyes because the Spirit had opened those eyes. I experienced Spirit-empowered preaching as the Holy Spirit gave me faith to receive His Word with blessing. That is why this book was written so Glory to God alone.

INTRODUCTION

The nature of the relationship between the Spirit of God and the Word of God has been debated among believers for centuries. How do the Word of God and Spirit of God relate in the inspiration of Scripture? What role does the Word have in regeneration in light of Peter's claim that his readers have been 'born again...through the living and abiding word of God' (1 Pet. 1:23) and James' reminder that God 'brought us forth by the word of truth' (James 1:18)? And what is the relationship between the Spirit of God and the Word of God in preaching? Is the Spirit present wherever and whenever the Word is preached?

This book focuses on that latter question. The question, of course, already begs a further question about what we mean when say that the Spirit is present. 1 Thessalonians 1:5 is a key text; Paul reminds the Thessalonians that 'our gospel came to you not only in word, but also in power and in the Holy Spirit and with full conviction.' Does this imply that the Word can be preached without the Holy Spirit? If so, is Paul speaking about the Spirit's influence on the preacher, his illumination of the hearers, his working of miracles to accompany the preached Word, or the very presence of the Spirit?[1]

Martyn Lloyd-Jones cited texts such as 1 Thessalonnians 1:5 in support of his doctrine of unction, urging that the Spirit sometimes accompanies the preached Word and sometimes does not.[2] He claimed that, throughout church history, 'the power came, and the power was withdrawn.'[3] Lloyd-Jones suggested that such fluctuations were clearly visible in the person of the preacher and the nature of his preaching. When a preacher is 'clothed with power and authority' he will be given 'clarity of thought, clarity of speech, ease of utterance, a great sense of authority and confidence.'[4] His people will notice the difference immediately and be gripped, convicted, moved and humbled. Lloyd-Jones counselled his readers to seek such accompaniment of the Spirit:

> Seek Him! Seek Him!…Let Him loose you, let Him manifest His power in you and through you. I am certain, as I have said several times before, that nothing but a return of this power of the Spirit on our preaching is going to avail us anything…This 'unction', this 'anointing', is the supreme thing. Seek it until you have it, be content with nothing less.[5]

Both Lloyd-Jones and contemporary writers draw evidence for this periodic empowerment and accompaniment of the Spirit from the history of revivals. Lloyd-Jones begins with Luther

---

1   For a discussion of the possibilities see: F. F. Bruce, *1 & 2 Thessalonians*, Word Biblical Commentary 45 (Nashville, TN: Thomas Nelson, 1982), 14; Charles A Wanamaker, *The Epistles to the Thessalonians*. (Grand Rapids, MI: Eerdmans, 1990), 79–80.

2   For a different reading of Lloyd-Jones see: Eryl Davies, *The Bala Conference* (Darlington: Evangelical Press, 2014).

3   D. Martyn Lloyd-Jones, *Preaching and Preachers* (London: Hodder and Stoughton, 1971), 324.

4   Ibid.

5   Ibid., 325.

and Calvin and ends with the preaching of David Morgan in the 1859 Welsh revival.[6] Robert Strivens asks his readers why Jonathan Edwards' famous sermon, 'Sinners in the Hand of an Angry God', yielded such emphatic results in Enfield and yet was preached on several other occasions with no such extraordinary effects.[7] The conclusion he draws is that the Spirit sometimes accompanies the preached Word by filling the preacher and sometimes does not.[8]

My purpose in writing this book is not to examine the topic from the perspective of biblical or systematic theology—enquiring what Scripture teaches. Nor is it to provide a full-blown analysis of Lloyd-Jones' understanding of the relationship between Word and Spirit in preaching or his claim that this is borne out by the evidence of church history. Rather, I want to examine the narrow historical theological question of what the Protestant Reformers, in particular John Calvin, actually taught on this topic. Several contemporary authors have claimed that Calvin not only distinguished Word and Spirit but separated them. This book seeks to assess whether that view is supported by the primary sources.

At the outset, it is helpful to make a couple of methodological observations about how we 'do' historical study. When researching the history of ideas it is crucial to understand what particular writers are trying to achieve by their words.[9] We must beware of the danger of what Quentin Skinner calls 'the priority of paradigms.' Skinner explains: '[T]he current historical study of ethical, political, religious, and other such modes of thought

---

6   Ibid., 315–323.

7   Robert Strivens, 'Preaching—'Ex Opere Operato?,'' in *The Truth Shall Make You Free*, ed. Roger Fay (Stoke: Tentmaker Publications, 2008), 57.

8   Strivens, 'Preaching,' 71; Lloyd-Jones, *Preaching and Preachers*, 324.

9   Quentin Skinner, 'Meaning and Understanding in the History of Ideas,' in *Visions of Politics. Vol.1: Regarding Method* (Cambridge: Cambridge University Press, 2002), 82–85.

is contaminated by the unconscious application of paradigms the familiarity of which, to the historian, disguises an essential inapplicability to the past.'[10] In the discipline of historical theology there is an acute danger of reading the heroes of the faith through the lens of our own theological and cultural convictions. We anachronistically treat them as if they were addressing and contributing to debates which post-date them by many centuries and which they show little if any awareness of.[11] The danger is particularly acute when assessing the views of the Protestant Reformers on the topic at hand because the views of the Reformed and Lutheran traditions have become hardened with time. The responsible historian needs to be alert to this danger and must acknowledge that it is impossible to come to a text without bringing one's own expectations, presuppositions and biases about what will be found there.

The historical theologian must also be careful not to assume coherence and consistency in the primary texts they are studying. It is quite possible that the author has not provided a coherent closed system of thought and the interpreter must not be blind to statements that contradict each other in the interests of revealing a supposed coherence.[12] The way we treat a theologian's work is quite different to the way we interpret Scripture where coherence and consistency are assumed since it is the very Word of God. We must be alert to complexities, nuances and the possibility of irreconcilable statements. If we are not, we will end up misreading the author's work and failing to understand the force of what they have actually written.

With those two methodological cautions in place, we can turn to the structure of this book. In the first chapter, the views of Philip Eveson, Robert Strivens, Stuart Olyott and Hywel Jones are

10   Ibid., 59.
11   Ibid., 60–62.
12   Ibid., 70.

introduced. These authors argue against a perceived conflation of Word and Spirit in contemporary preaching and suggest that it is a significant departure from the Reformed tradition in general and Calvin in particular. In the second chapter, we consider the diversity of views held upon the topic by the radical Reformers, Martin Luther, Huldyrch Zwingli and Heinrich Bullinger. The churchmen are considered in this order since their views are, to a certain (although often over-stated) extent, reactive to one another. The third and fourth chapters provide a critical exposition of Calvin's views, examining first Calvin's sacramental theology and then providing a critical exposition of his views on the relationship between Word and Spirit as found in the *Institutes*, Calvin's commentaries and his other writings. The important connections between his understanding of preaching and the other means of grace are noted. In the conclusion I will make some brief observations about the trajectory of later developments in the Reformed and Lutheran traditions and consider the significance of Calvin's teaching for preaching and church life.

1

THE CURRENT CONTROVERSY

Since 2006, four articles have been published in the United Kingdom addressing the relationship between Word and Spirit in preaching. They share a common point of reference in seeking to combat what the authors perceive to be a growing tendency in the evangelical church to marginalise the role of the Spirit in the work of preaching. They claim that what is happening is a distortion of the classic Reformed understanding of the relationship between Word and Spirit and caution about where it may lead the church.

A CRITIQUE OF MOORE THEOLOGY

The first article, authored by Philip Eveson is titled "Moore Theology': A Friendly Critique'. It was published in the Autumn 2006 issue of *Foundations*, the theological journal of Affinity and was the product of papers delivered at the Westminster Fellowship of Gospel Preachers, London, and the Bala Ministers' Conference earlier that year. [1] Eveson had been asked to address the teaching

---

1 Philip H. Eveson, "Moore Theology': A Friendly Critique,' *Foundations* (2006): 18–30.

and influence of Moore Theological College, Sydney.[2] The article is wide-ranging, introducing Moore's history and contemporary influence and addressing topics such as Moore's understanding of the 'Call', the 'Ministry', worship, the Mosaic Law, and revival. It was deliberately narrow and pastoral since Eveson wished to address the strong influence that Moore was having on pastors, students and some church members in the UK.[3]

Eveson has three central criticisms of Moore's theology. Firstly, he suggests that its emphasis upon biblical theology results in the marginalisation of historical and systematic theology, leading Moore College astray in several key areas. Secondly, he contends that Moore's 'repugnance of all things charismatic' causes them to underemphasise the Spirit's activity in the church and in the individual believer.[4] Thirdly, he argues that Moore has a low view of the church leading them into pragmatism on the matter of mixed congregations.[5]

In places, Eveson's methodology for determining what constitutes Moore's theology is rather questionable. He focuses almost entirely upon articles published in *The Briefing*, a monthly periodical published in the UK by 'The Good Book Company'. While *The Briefing's* founder, Philip Jensen, and editor, Tony Payne, studied at Moore College, the periodical has no formal links to the college. Of the articles Eveson cites, almost all of them are written by former students of Moore, and only a few by Faculty. Moreover, Eveson's claim that books written by Vaughan Roberts and Peter and Ann Woodcock represent Moore Theology is unsustainable.[6] Neither Roberts nor the Woodcocks were

---

2   See ibid., 30, n 1.

3   Philip Eveson wished to stress this in email correspondence about the article, 7th May 2014.

4   Ibid., 25.

5   Ibid., 29.

6   Ibid., 22, n. 9; 27, n. 25.

trained at Moore College and neither have any formal association with the college.

Fortunately, the topic of particular interest to us, the relationship between Word and Spirit, is not affected by this methodological problem, since the author who Eveson focuses on is Moore's former principal, John Woodhouse.[7] Eveson cites three articles written by Woodhouse in early issues of *The Briefing*.[8] In the first, Woodhouse traces the prominence of the Word of God throughout redemptive history, concluding: 'Our whole practice and experience of Christianity flows from this reality: that God has spoken. Everything—and I mean everything—is a consequence of that reality.' Eveson states that he shares Woodhouse's emphasis upon the importance of the Word of God and warms to his insistence that the Word should be central to what Christians do as they gather together. He cautions, however, that Woodhouse draws false deductions from this firm foundation: he suggests that 'because Christians already have the Spirit all that is needed is to have gifted men who will faithfully preach and teach the Word.' According to Eveson, Woodhouse neglects the fact that Christians can receive faithful sermons by gifted preachers and yet still remain 'dry, dull and dead.'[9]

Eveson proceeds to Woodhouse's second article which addresses the relationship between Word and Spirit more directly. He notes that Woodhouse is concerned to respond to those who question where 'experience' fits into his framework and who feel

7   John Woodhouse retired in 2013 and was succeeded by Mark Thompson.

8   John Woodhouse, 'The God of Word,' *The Briefing*, September 1988, matthiasmedia.com.au/briefing/library/1297/; John Woodhouse, 'Word and Spirit: The God of Word II,' *The Briefing*, September 1988, matthiasmedia.com.au/briefing/library/1299/; John Woodhouse, 'Word and Bible: The God of Word III,' *The Briefing*, October 1988, matthiasmedia.com.au/briefing/library/1304/. Woodhouse later assimilated and developed his material in a contribution to a collection of essays: C. Green and David Jackman, eds., *When God's Voice Is Heard* (Leicester: IVP, 1995).

9   Eveson, 'Moore Theology,' 27.

that his 'narrow emphasis on the *word* is at the expense of the *Spirit*'. He acknowledges that Woodhouse primarily has charismatics in view but expresses concern about where Woodhouse's argument might lead. Woodhouse's aim is to emphasise the close connection between the Word of God and the Spirit of God in the Bible. He begins by pointing out the broad semantic range of *rûaḥ* and *pneuma* (the Hebrew and Greek words often translated spirit) noting that '[t]hroughout the Bible, the Spirit of God is as closely connected to the Word of God as *breath* is connected to *speech*.' He then develops this by reflecting on some texts including Genesis 1:1–3, Isaiah 11:2, 59:21, 61:1, Luke 4:18, Matthew 10:16–20, Acts 1:8, 5:30–32.

It is in his handling of 1 Thessalonnians 1:4–6 and Romans 8:16 that Eveson takes particular exception. Woodhouse references the former and comments: 'Are there two things going on here— "not only in word but also in power and in the Holy Spirit"? No, he is describing one experience: what they experienced "when our gospel came". The gospel is never just words.'[10] Eveson disagrees, insisting that there are two things taking place in 1 Thessalonnians 1:5: 'there is the human speech of the apostles and there is the convincing power of the Holy Spirit.'[11]

They disagree again on Romans 8:16 where Woodhouse argues that, in common with other passages in the New Testament, Paul refers here to 'the subjective effect of the Spirit's work.' The question is *how* the Spirit testifies to us; and according to Woodhouse it is 'by the gospel, by the word of God!' Woodhouse concludes:

> Where there is the word *of God*, there certainly is the Holy Spirit. After all, it is his sword. The Christian life is fully lived in the power of the Spirit, not when something additional to the word of God is discovered and called a spiritual gift, but when, and only when,

10   Ibid., 28.
11   Ibid.

the word of God is at work in you who believe—when God, by his Spirit, *addresses* us and we receive *his* word.[12]

In context, Woodhouse's comments are clearly directed at those of a charismatic persuasion who would argue that there are revelatory spiritual gifts which supplement Scripture; but Eveson opposes the comments because they leave no room 'for unction, for some special anointing on preacher or people.' Woodhouse's exegesis, according to Eveson, is 'typical of the way Moore men operate' and 'no commentator worth his salt' exegetes the passage in the way that Woodhouse does.[13] Eveson presents John Murray's commentary as evidence for the contrary view, in which Murray distinguishes between the witness 'borne *by* the believer's own consciousness in virtue of the Holy Spirit's indwelling as the spirit of adoption' in verse 15 and 'the witness borne by the Holy Spirit himself' in verse 16.[14] The problem with Eveson's attempt to marshal Murray in support of his cause is that Murray is discussing an entirely different issue. He is distinguishing between the believer's own spirit-empowered consciousness that testifies to his sonship and the indwelling spirit himself who testifies to the same. The two witnesses work 'conjointly,' Murray insists, but they must be 'distinguished.'[15] They are distinct but not separate. Woodhouse discusses a quite different question, namely, whether the Spirit operates without means in this testifying work. 'How does the Spirit testify?' Woodhouse asks.[16] Is he a second witness

12   Woodhouse, 'Word and Spirit.'

13   Eveson, 'Moore Theology,' 28.

14   John Murray, *The Epistle to the Romans*, New International Commentary of the New Testament (Grand Rapids, MI: Eerdmans, 1959), 297.

15   Ibid.

16   This is not to suggest that the Spirit acts through 'facts and arguments alone' (Douglas J Moo, *The Epistle to the Romans*, The New International Commentary on the New Testament [Grand Rapids, MI: William B. Eerdmans, 1996], 502).

operating independently and separate from the witness of the Word? Woodhouse replies in the negative and Murray agrees: 'We are not to construe this witness of the Spirit as consisting in a direct propositional revelation to the effect, 'Thou art a child of God'.' Rather the witness is borne in many respects and primarily through 'sealing to the hearts of believers the promises which are theirs as heirs of God and joint heirs with Christ.'[17] In other words, the Spirit primarily performs his subjective work in the believer by confirming the objective promises of the Word.

Eveson concludes his critique by endorsing Woodhouse's concern to emphasise the Bible as the sole source of authority but argues that he has gone too far in so identifying 'word and Spirit that the Spirit has no separate identity and function'.[18] It is a little difficult to ascertain the precise substance of Eveson's objection. Is he arguing that Woodhouse and Moore College so emphasise the Word that the Spirit ceases to exist within their theology as a distinct trinitarian person? If so, this is a serious accusation to make and he has not made the case adequately. Alternatively, is Eveson claiming that a failure to adequately distinguish between Word and Spirit has led to a mixture and confusion of the two? This is possible but Eveson's language, referring to a 'separate' identity, a 'direct work of the Spirit' and the 'need to pray for unction' suggests that his concern is at a different level.[19] He regrets Moore's failure to separate Word and Spirit and refusal to affirm that the Word can be present without the Spirit. He deems this to be 'a serious departure from the Puritan and Evangelical teaching of the past.'[20] While this is a general claim rather than a specific (he does not name Calvin or explicitly claim that Moore follows Luther on this point), it is clear that Eveson considers

---

17   Murray, *The Epistle to the Romans*, 279–280.

18   Eveson, 'Moore Theology,' 28.

19   Ibid., 28–29.

20   Ibid., 28.

Moore to be stepping outside the bounds of the Reformed and Evangelical heritage that it claims to defend.[21]

A final word is appropriate concerning the blunt and imprecise language that both Eveson and Woodhouse use in their articles. The differences in this debate are slight in their articulation but far-reaching in their consequences. Therefore it is important to be precise in our enunciation, just as it was in the fourth and fifth century debates concerning the Trinity and Christology. In his discussion of 1 Thessalonnians 1:5, Woodhouse asks, 'Are there two things going on here?…No, [Paul] is describing one experience: what they experienced "when our gospel came". The gospel is never just words.'[22] The problem with this reasoning is that there can, of course, be more than one thing 'going on' in a single experience. As I sit here listening to my children play downstairs, I have one sensory experience—that of hearing—which my nervous system communicates to my brain via my eardrum, impacted by sound waves emanating from my three children. I have one experience but numerous persons, instruments and means contribute to it. It is a logical fallacy to suggest that if there is a single experience there can only be one thing 'going on.'

Secondly, both Woodhouse and Eveson fail to adequately distinguish between the concepts of distinction and separation. Woodhouse is so determined to oppose those who argue for a supplementary source of authority that he appears (at least) to conflate Word and Spirit, viewing them as virtually synonymous. Eveson, on the other hand, falls into the opposite error, assuming that because Word and Spirit are distinct they must necessarily be separate. Both would have been aided by the vocabulary of the Trinitarian and Christological debates to which we will return in due course.

---

21   For Moore's Protestant and evangelical credentials see: Ibid., 18–20.
22   Woodhouse, 'Word and Spirit.'

PREACHING – 'EX OPERE OPERATO?'

While Eveson only made the general claim that Moore's understanding of Word and Spirit marks 'a serious departure from the
Puritan and Evangelical teaching of the past', Robert Strivens
makes a more specific claim in his contribution to the 2007
Westminster Conference. His paper is motivated by a concern
that there are 'evangelicals today…who want to play down the
independent role of the Spirit in the proclamation of the Word,
and who want to argue that this Spirit is at work inevitably,
whenever the Word is expounded aright.'[23] Strivens argues that
this is a Lutheran view which has significant consequences for
preaching, preachers and church life. The paper (which provides
the most detailed and rigorous historical analysis of the four
considered here) is divided into four sections. The first two are
historical while the latter two deal with exegetical issues and the
practical consequences of the debate. I will sketch out Strivens'
arguments in brief and return to them in the following chapters.

The first section deals with the conception of Word and Spirit
held by Luther and the Swiss Reformers. Strivens argues that
Luther's views in this area were decisively influenced by the
reforms instituted at Wittenberg by Karlstadt and the visit of the
Zwickau Prophets in late 1521. Strivens notes that in 1521 Luther
could speak of people receiving 'understanding immediately from
the Holy Spirit,'[24] but by 1525 he was insisting that the outward
receipt of the gospel through word and sacrament must precede
the inward receipt through the Holy Spirit, faith and other
gifts.[25] He suggests that this binding 'together…[of] the work of
the Spirit and the means of grace, including the preaching of the

---

23   Strivens, 'Preaching,' 71.

24   Luther's exposition of the Magnificat in Luke 1: Ibid., 60.

25   Ibid. Strivens cites Luther's treatise 'Against the Heavenly Prophets' as
cited in Bernhard Lohse, *Martin Luther's Theology: Its Historical and Systematic
Development* (Edinburgh: T&T Clark, 1999), 148.

Word'[26] was a reaction against the 'enthusiasts,' citing Hans Denck as an exemplar. Strivens suggests this led Luther to tie the Spirit and the Word together in an 'indissoluble bond.' '[T]he outward means of grace were essential in Luther's thinking' Strivens writes and, for Luther, 'Word and Spirit always work together, never apart.'[27] This view, he writes, was formalised in Article V of the *Augsburg Confession* (1530) and Article III of the *Formula of Concord* (1577). Strivens' reading of Luther is based upon a limited number of sources (which is inevitable given the size and breadth of scope of the article) and does not fully trace out how the context may have shaped Luther's comments. As we shall see in the following chapter, Luther's thinking on the relationship between Word and Spirit was extremely complex and carried a tension throughout, which probably cannot be resolved simply by reference to a perceived development of thought following the events at Wittenberg in 1521.

Strivens deals with the Swiss Reformers more briefly. He begins with Zwingli and Bullinger noting that, like Luther, they denied the possibility of fresh revelation but unlike the German they refused to tie together Word and Spirit. While maintaining that the Spirit was required to rightly understand and apply the Word, they insisted that 'the Spirit was given directly to the believer for this purpose and was not tied to Scripture in the way that Luther appeared to teach.'[28] Strivens refers to Luther's criticisms of the Swiss Reformers as recorded in *Table-Talk* and suggests that Luther wrongly 'lump[s] together' the Swiss Reformers and the Enthusiasts when in fact the Reformers occupied a middle ground 'insisting on the centrality of the Word and refusing all claims to new revelation, and yet maintaining that God was able, if he so wished to withhold the blessing of his Spirit from his

26 Strivens, 'Preaching,' 61.
27 Ibid., 62.
28 Ibid., 63.

Word, and indeed to work by his Spirit apart from the Word.'[29]
We will consider whether this is a fair representation of the views
of Zwingli and Bullinger in the next chapter.

Strivens provides a more extended treatment of Calvin who,
he claims, insisted that 'the preacher may rightly expect the Spirit
to be at work when the Word is preached' but balanced this by
saying that the 'Spirit is not absolutely bound to the Word.'[30]
Support for this proposition is given from Calvin's commentary
on 2 Corinthians 3:6 where Paul is said to deny that 'the grace
and power of the Holy Spirit are so bound to his preaching
that he could, whenever he wished, breathe out the Spirit along
with the words that he spoke.'[31] Strivens also points to Calvin's
commentary on Isaiah 35:4 in which he affirmed the efficacy
of the Word but insisted that this did not mean that the Word
operates 'always or indiscriminately, but where it pleases God by
the secret power of his Spirit.'[32] Strivens urges that just as Calvin
held that the Spirit does not necessarily give efficacy to the Word,
so he allowed for the operation of the Spirit without the Word
on occasion, pointing to Calvin's commentary on Matthew 15:23
(Christ's encounter with a Canaanite woman) and Amos 4:12–13.
Strivens concludes: 'Calvin believed in a very close relationship
between Word and Spirit, but did not tie the two together
irrevocably.' God is able to work 'by his Spirit apart from the
Word' and the Word can be preached 'in a manner that is bereft
of the Spirit.'[33]

29   Ibid.

30   Ibid., 64.

31   John Calvin, *The Second Epistle of Paul the Apostle to the Corinthians and
the Epistles to Timothy, Titus and Philemon*, ed. David W. Torrance and Thomas
F. Torrance, trans. T. A. Smail (Edinburgh: Oliver and Boyd, 1964), 43. Cited
in Strivens, 'Preaching,' 64.

32   John Calvin, *Commentary on the Book of the Prophet Isaiah: Volume 3*,
trans. William Pringle (Edinburgh: Calvin Translation Society, 1852), 65. Cited
in Strivens, 'Preaching,' 64.

33   Strivens, 'Preaching,' 65.

Several observations are appropriate. Firstly, Strivens' reading of Calvin is based upon a relatively small number of primary texts (which again is inevitable given the size and breadth of the article) and there is little interaction with material that is more difficult to accommodate within his schema (which we will consider in chapter four). Secondly, Strivens does not identify the connections between Word and Sacrament in Calvin's thinking and this, in turn, means that he overlooks a crucial matrix for understanding Calvin's thinking on the relationship between Word and Spirit. Thirdly, much like Woodhouse and Eveson before him, Strivens does not distinguish between the concepts of distinction and separation and assumes that because Word and Spirit are distinguished they must also be separated. Fourthly, it is possible that at points he falls into the methodological trap of the 'priority of paradigms', reading his own context into Calvin. This seems to have happened in his claim that, for Calvin, 'the Word can be preached in a *manner* that is bereft of the Spirit and which renders it thereby a "dead letter".'[34] While this conclusion fits well with Strivens' own thesis that a conflation of Word and Spirit negatively impacts upon sermon preparation and communication style, there is no evidence of these concerns occupying the mind of Calvin in the material cited. We will return to these observations in our more detailed consideration of Calvin in chapters three and four.

In the second section of his paper, Strivens considers how the Reformed and Lutheran views of the relationship between Word and Spirit developed post-Reformation. On the Reformed side, he notes that Charles Hodge sharply distinguished his own view from that of the Lutherans.[35] Strivens also quotes from

34   Ibid. (emphasis added).

35   Ibid., 66. For Hodge's discussion of the Lutheran view, see Charles Hodge, *Systematic Theology*, vol. III (Peabody, MA: Hendrickson Publishers Inc, 2003), 479–485.

George Smeaton's nineteenth century work, *The Doctrine of the Holy Spirit*, in which Smeaton emphasises the importance of distinguishing between Christ's omnipresence, which is a fact and not a promise, and Christ's 'gracious presence' with his church by the Spirit. Just as the Lutherans have failed to observe this important distinction in their doctrine of the ubiquity of Christ's humanity, so too they have failed to see that '[i]t is God's sovereignty that determines when and to what extent the preaching of the gospel is accompanied by his blessing.'[36]

In his discussion of the Lutheran view, Strivens quotes from John Theodore Mueller's twentieth century work, *Christian Dogmatics: A Handbook of Doctrinal Theology for Pastors, Teachers, and Laymen.*[37] He notes that Mueller distinguishes the Lutheran scheme from that of the Reformed, insisting that the Word 'by its truly divine power...actually converts, regenerates, and renews...The divine efficacy of Scripture is nothing else than God's power in the Word.'[38] Strivens suggests that this represents a 'sharpening of the doctrine' when compared with Luther but that Mueller follows Luther in emphasising the importance of the external means of grace. Both Luther and Mueller teach that 'God invariably works through such means' and thus when 'the Word is preached, the means of grace are brought to all who hear.'[39] Strivens suggests that this view is confronted by a major problem in that it fails to account for why some hearers are benefited by the preaching of the Word while others are not.

---

36   Strivens, 'Preaching,' 66. Referring to: George Smeaton, *The Doctrine of the Holy Spirit.* (London: Banner of Truth Trust, 1958), Lecture VI.

37   John Theodore Mueller, *Christian Dogmatics: A Handbook of Doctrinal Theology for Pastors, Teachers, and Laymen* (St. Louis, MO: Concordia Publishing House, 1955).

38   Cited in Strivens, 'Preaching,' 67.

39   Ibid., 68.

Mueller fails to resolve this problem insisting instead that it is 'a mystery not to be enquired into.'[40]

Strivens provides a helpful and concise summary of the differences between contemporary Reformed and Lutheran views on the topic. Unfortunately its brevity is also its problem. While acknowledging that Mueller departs from Luther in some important respects, Strivens does not investigate this more fully. On the Reformed side, he argues that 'Calvin's view' has been 'consistently held by Reformed theologians from Calvin's time to our own.'[41] This is unlikely given the progress of theology,[42] and it overlooks the significant developments that took place in the intervening period in Reformed sacramental theology. Given the connections that Strivens notes between one's understanding of the presence of Christ in the sacraments and one's understanding of the relationship between Word and Spirit in preaching, it is likely that further exploration of this line of thought would have yielded fruit.

In the third section of his paper, Strivens looks at the relationship between the Word and Spirit in preaching from a systematic and exegetical perspective. He helpfully states what he perceives to be the central point at issue: 'Has God so ordained it that the Spirit is somehow inherent in the Word, inseparable from it, inevitably present and at work whenever the Word is rightly preached? Or does the Spirit work alongside and in tandem with the Word, but not necessarily inseparably from it?'[43] He posits that, in defence of their view, the Lutherans would point to Romans 1:16; 10:17; John 6:63; 1 Corinthians 2:4 and 1 Thessalonnians 1:5. The Reformed, according to Strivens, would answer that the verses from Romans and John's Gospel merely state that the Word is

40   Ibid.

41   Ibid., 65.

42   See James Orr, *The Progress of Dogma* (London: James Clarke & Co, 1901), 1–32.

43   Strivens, 'Preaching,' 69.

efficacious; they do not explain how that efficacy is given to the Word and therefore do not address the point at issue. The other verses simply deal with Paul's experience on particular occasions. They do not set down a theological principle which is applicable to all preaching, everywhere and in every situation.[44] Strivens adds that there are other passages which 'surely demonstrate that the preaching of the Word is sometimes accompanied by the Spirit in great power, and sometimes not.'[45] The passages he points to are Peter's speeches in Acts 2 and 4 in which Peter is said to be 'filled with the Spirit' and after which many are said to be converted; and Paul's address to the Areopagus in Acts 17. Strivens writes: 'Surely this suggests that the power of the Spirit is to be thought of, not so much as being inherent in the Word preached, but in the preacher doing the preaching.'[46]

We cannot undertake a detailed assessment of Strivens' exegesis here and our primary concern is historical rather than exegetical. Nevertheless, it is appropriate to make a few observations. Firstly, Strivens does not provide a detailed defence of his own reading of Romans 1:16; 10:17; John 6:63; 1 Corinthians 2:4 and 1 Thessalonnians 1:5; he simply points out that an alternative reading is plausible. Secondly, the passages he cites to reinforce his own position are not persuasive. At root, it appears to be an argument from silence: because Acts 17 does not state that Paul was 'filled with the Spirit' we must assume that he was not and that this explains why his preaching on this occasion was not accompanied by numerous conversions. Aside from the weaknesses of an argument from silence, the fact that 'some men' in Athens believed (v. 34) seems to undermine Strivens' point. If the work of the Spirit is 'essential in order to make the Word

44   Ibid., 70.
45   Ibid.
46   Ibid., 71.

effective,'[47] as all parties agree, then it is clear that the Spirit must have accompanied Paul's preaching in Athens since some of his hearers were converted.

In the final section, Strivens traces out the practical outworkings of this debate in contemporary evangelicalism. In so doing he appears to fall into the 'priority of paradigms' trap. He claims that, just like the Lutherans, there are 'evangelicals today...who want to play down the independent role of the Spirit in the proclamation of the Word.'[48] Strivens does not explicitly name these evangelicals but describes them as men whose 'focus will tend to be on ensuring that [they] rightly exegete the passage.'[49] They will consider their task as 'simply to open up the passage in a way that reflects faithfully the tenor and meaning of the passage in view – nothing more. If he does that, he does all that is required of him as preacher.'[50] Strivens argues that such a preacher will spend '[a]ll his time in preparation...ensuring that he has rightly understood the meaning and import of the passage.' As a result, compared with his Reformed contemporary, he will lack dependence on the sovereignty of God and his prayers will lack urgency and persistence. The problem here is that the exact opposite deduction could just as easily be made: the preacher who assumes such a limited role for himself will be all the more dependent upon God to do the rest.

Strivens ends his article with four pieces of practical advice for preachers who would seek to apply the Reformed understanding of Word and Spirit in preaching. Firstly, they should be utterly dependent on the Spirit, seeking his help: 'in our choice of passage, in our preparation and for the delivery and reception of the

47   Ibid., 69.

48   Ibid., 71.

49   This is a significant problem for anyone seeking to respond. Without Strivens naming the evangelicals he has in view, it is impossible to determine whether he is opposing a non-existent straw man.

50   Strivens, 'Preaching,' 71.

sermon itself.'[51] Secondly, the preacher 'must have a conscious, felt dependence upon the Spirit, both in preparation and in delivery.' Strivens suggests that prayer alone is insufficient for this. Thirdly, the preacher should crave true humility in his preaching. Fourthly, none of what has been said about the Reformed approach should be used as an excuse for poor preparation. God's ability to do as he wills does not diminish the preacher's responsibility for careful exegesis and thoughtful application.[52] Strivens concludes his advice by exhorting preachers to 'give [their] all to sermon preparation, and then go into the pulpit convinced that our all amounts to precisely zero in terms of efficacy.'[53] This is all excellent advice but it does not really touch upon the core concern of the article. All parties to the sixteenth century debate and, indeed, the twenty-first century debate would heartily endorse the statement since, as Strivens concedes, they all agree that 'the work of the Spirit is essential to make the Word effective.'[54] The real point at issue is the relationship between the Word and Spirit in preaching. Are they separate or are they distinct yet inseparable? Strivens' practical advice, at a general level at least, could be endorsed from either position.

WHERE LUTHER GOT IT WRONG

In September 2009, Stuart Olyott delivered the Dedication Service address at the Wales Evangelical School of Theology (WEST) and later published a modified version of the address in the *Banner of Truth Magazine*.[55] He used the opportunity to dispute Luther's famous claim that 'the Word did it all,' arguing

51   Alarmingly this could be taken to exclude on principle sequential expository preaching.
52   Strivens, 'Preaching,' 72–73.
53   Ibid., 73.
54   See ibid., 69.
55   'Where Luther Got It Wrong—and Why We Need to Know About It,' *The Banner of Truth*, no. 555 (December 2009): 25.

that Luther was wrong to attribute success to the Word. Olyott provided the following quotation of Luther:

> I opposed indulgences and all papists, but never by force. I simply taught, preached, wrote God's Word: otherwise I did nothing. And then, while I slept, or drank Wittenberg beer with my Philip of Amsdorf, the Word so greatly weakened the papacy that never a prince or emperor did such damage to it. I did nothing: the Word did it all. Had I wanted to start trouble…I could have started such a little game at Worms that even the emperor wouldn't have been safe. But what would it have been? A mug's game. I did nothing: I left it to the Word.[56]

According to Olyott, Luther's fundamental error was 'mediate' regeneration,[57] an error that was 'on the march once more' having already 'taken over vast sections of British Evangelicalism.'[58] It teaches that the Spirit uses an instrument—the Word—to bring about regeneration.[59] Olyott insists that this is contrary to the clear testimony of Scripture which teaches that while the Spirit often *accompanies* the Word he does not work *through* the Word. According to Olyott, regeneration takes place through the 'direct and immediate energy of the Holy Spirit…without using an instrument.'[60] Olyott anticipates possible objections, insisting that his view does not mean that God 'simply "zaps" people and they believe.' Rather, the Spirit gives people 'sight' so that 'what they see is the truth of the Word.' Olyott maintains that this is the position taught in Scripture, citing Acts 16:14 and 2 Corinthians 4:6 as key texts. He also addresses two texts that seem to point in the opposite direction, James 1:18 and 1 Peter 1:23, claiming that what they describe is not 'the act of germination

---

56 Ibid.

57 This terminology was popularised by Louis Berkhof (*Systematic Theology* [Edinburgh: Banner of Truth Trust, 1958], 474).

58 Olyott, 'Where Luther Got It Wrong,' 25.

59 Ibid., 26.

60 Ibid.

(where the new life comes into being) but…the moment of birth (where the new life becomes visible).'[61]

In his conclusion, Olyott contrasts two mind-sets which he considers to be prevalent in contemporary evangelicalism. The first mind-set emphasises 'Word ministry' and claims, 'As long as we sow the Word, concentrating on making its meaning clear, spiritual work will get done.'[62] The second is the 'biblical mind-set' and it 'ticks completely differently.' It produces preachers who strive and agonise in prayer until 'the Lord accompanies their preaching in an obvious way.' It gives rise to prayer meetings 'filled with believers who storm the throne of grace, determined that by sheer importunity they will persuade God to accompany the word to be preached.' And it generates earnest prayer for 'awakening power' and 'revival.'[63] This 'biblical mind-set' is what British Evangelicalism desperately needs according to Olyott. Instead of teaching that the 'Word did it all' it teaches that God *may* 'accompany his Word' and that we must plead with him to do so.

We must restrict ourselves to a few observations. Firstly, Olyott repeats Strivens' claim that there is a significant but unidentified section of British Evangelicalism which adopts a Lutheran approach to Word and Spirit in preaching with deleterious effects. Secondly, unlike Strivens, he bases his assessment upon a single text from Luther which he cites without providing its source or context.[64] This is problematic because the surrounding context makes clear that Luther is not directly addressing the issue of

---

61   Ibid., 28.

62   Ibid.

63   Ibid., 29.

64   He also misquotes the passage fusing Philip (referring to Philip Melancthon) and Amsdorf (referring to Nicholas von Amsdorf).See critique of Olyott's methodology in George M. Ella, 'Where Olyott Got It Wrong,' *Biographia Evangelica*, accessed August 22, 2011, evangelica.de/articles/where-olyott-got-it-wrong/. These methodological problems do not of course affect the overall flow and force of Olyott's argument.

the relationship between Word and Spirit but is focussed on the narrower point of the radical Reformers' attempts to abolish the Mass. As we shall see in chapter two, Luther most certainly did not teach that the preaching of the Word yields fruit apart from God's work. In fact, he makes the exact opposite claim in the Invocavit sermon to which Olyott refers.

Thirdly, Olyott's exegesis which is based upon Louis Bekhof's *Systematic Theology* is strained in places.[65] To defend his position from Acts 16:14, he provides his own translation of the verse: 'whose heart the Lord opened by a single act, with the result that she heeded to the things being spoken by Paul.' Olyott renders the aorist active verb διήνοιξεν (*diēnoixen*, opened up completely) in a passive sense and over-translates, adding 'by a single act.' This supports Olyott's own position but is not to be found in the original. Moreover, contrary to the impression that Olyott presents, the Greek does not exclude the use of means in this opening work.[66]

Olyott's treatment of James 1:18 and 1 Peter 1:23 is ingenious but ultimately unconvincing. [67] The verb used in the former verse, ἀποκυέω (*apokyeō*), clearly refers to birth rather than conception,[68] but the verb used in the latter ἀναγεννάω (*anagennaō*), has a broader semantic range. The uncompounded form is used in Matthew 1:20 to describe Jesus' conception and the compounded form is found in John 3:5 to describe regeneration. Therefore, Olyott's distinction between germination and birth

---

65 Berkhof, *Systematic Theology*, 473–476.

66 See critique of Ella in 'Where Olyott Got It Wrong.'

67 See also: Berkhof, *Systematic Theology*, 475.

68 *BDAG* gives the following senses: 'a. of delivery of that with which one has been pregnant…b. otherwise in our lit. only fig., *hē hamartia a. thanaton* sin gives birth to (i.e. brings forth) death Js 1:15.' William Arndt, Frederick W. Danker, and Walter Bauer, eds., *A Greek-English Lexicon of the New Testament and Other Early Christian Literature*, 3rd ed. (Chicago: University of Chicago Press, 2000).

in regeneration is not one found in Scripture and his case is not advanced by it.

Fourthly, we should note that the real point at issue in Olyott's article is not mediate regeneration but the relationship between Word and Spirit in preaching.[69] Mediate regeneration is something of a red herring. As Sinclair Ferguson has observed, the use of means does not undermine the Spirit's monergistic and sovereign activity in regeneration:

> For the New Testament writers…there is no hint of a threat to divine sovereignty in the fact that the word is the instrumental cause of regeneration, while the Spirit is the efficient cause. This is signalled in the New Testament by the use of the preposition *ek* to indicate the divine originating cause (*e.g.* Jn 3:5; 1 Jn 3:9; 5:1) and *dia* to express the instrumental cause (*e.g.* Jn 15:3; 1 Cor 4:15; 1 Pet 1:23).[70]

Olyott, like Eveson and Strivens before him, is concerned to oppose those who would conflate the Word and Spirit in preaching. His proposal is to separate Word and Spirit so that the Spirit may on occasion accompany the Word and on other occasions may not. Like his contemporaries, Olyott does not consider the possibility that Word and Spirit might be distinct yet inseparable in preaching.

PREACHING THE WORD IN THE POWER OF THE SPIRIT

Hywel Jones contributed a paper to the Affinity Theological Studies conference in 2010 which was later published in *Founda-*

---

69   See: Guy Davies, 'Mediate Regeneration,' *Exiled Preacher*, last modified January 13, 2010, accessed August 22, 2011, exiledpreacher.blogspot.com/2010/01/mediate-reneneration.html.

70   Sinclair B. Ferguson, *The Holy Spirit* (Leicester: IVP, 1996), 125. See also: Iain Campbell, 'Word and Spirit—a Theological Orientation,' *Foundations* 39 (1997): 4.

tions titled 'Preaching the Word in the Power of the Holy Spirit.'[71] In the paper he seeks to trace out the relationship between Word and Spirit in preaching. Because he covers much of the same ground as previous publications we can deal with his contribution more briefly.

Jones begins his paper by identifying four foundations for the task of preaching from 2 Corinthians 4:1–7. These are helpful but not of immediate relevance to the present discussion. In the following section he laments the absence of discussion of the Holy Spirit in recent publications on preaching, highlighting two collections of essays.[72] Jones writes: 'There is not much of an emphasis at all on praying for the Holy Spirit's power to descend on the ministry of the word and on the preacher and hearer alike. This is a tell-tale sign. Is this superfluous now that we have the whole Bible and the skill to interpret any passage of it? Or is it doctrinally unacceptable?'[73]

In the eighth section of his paper, Jones discusses the disagreement between the sixteenth century Reformers concerning the relationship between Word and Spirit. He references Murray: 'It is a persistently recurring question whether the Holy Spirit works in the believer only in by or through the Scripture or whether the Spirit works sometimes independently of the Scripture. Is the Spirit tied to Scripture?'[74] We ought to note that this is a different question to the one previously asked by Eveson, Strivens and Olyott which was whether the Word can be preached without

71   Hywel R. Jones, 'Preaching the Word in the Power of the Holy Spirit,' *Foundations* 60 (2011): 71–90.

72   Samuel T. Logan, *Preaching: The Preacher and Preaching in the Twentieth Century* (Welwyn: Evangelical Press, 1986); C. Green and David Jackman, eds., *When God's Voice Is Heard* (Leicester: IVP, 1995).

73   Jones, 'Preaching the Word,' 75.

74   John Murray, 'Review of The Holy Spirit in Puritan Faith and Experience by G.F. Nuttal,' in *Collected Writings of John Murray Vol. 3 Life of John Murray, Sermons & Reviews* (Edinburgh: Banner of Truth Trust, 1982), 325. Cited in Jones, 'Preaching the Word,' 79.

the accompaniment of the Spirit. As evidence of the continuing nature of the debate, Jones refers to the views of Herman Bavinck, Charles Hodge and John Woodhouse. We have already considered the views of Woodhouse and Hodge earlier in this chapter, and we will return to Bavinck in the conclusion. It suffices to note at this point that Bavinck adopted a position much closer to Calvin than either Hodge or Woodhouse.

Jones summarises Bavinck and Hodge uncritically and seemingly not identifying any differences between their views. His tack changes when he comes to Woodhouse whom he argues 'repeatedly collapses the Spirit's work into the meaning of the Word.' Jones aligns Woodhouse with Luther citing Olyott's article. He suggests that 'Luther's well known statement… should not be considered as if it were a doctrinal definition,'[75] and contrasts it with the view of Calvin using a short quotation from Calvin's commentary on Ezekiel. Jones then subjects Woodhouse's exegesis of 1 Thessalonnians 1:4–6 and Romans 8:16 to a critique similar to the one presented by Eveson five years earlier.

Jones concludes his paper by affirming that the Word is conjoined to the Spirit and must never be disconnected from it but that the Spirit is 'greater' than the Word and must not be imprisoned in it. By this he means that the Spirit 'works where he wills and as he wills, but in differing degrees of might as it pleases him.'[76] Jones continues with a brief excursus in defence of the 'internal call'[77] and against manuscripts, auto-cues, handouts and projectors. It is not entirely clear how this fits with

---

75   Jones, 'Preaching the Word,' 82.

76   Ibid., 83.

77   Jones is concerned about its denial or omission in recent works on preaching: Colin Marshall and Tony Payne, *The Trellis and the Vine: The Ministry Mind-Shift That Changes Everything* (Kingsford: Matthias Media, 2009), 129–134; Christopher Ash, *The Priority of Preaching* (Fearn: Christian Focus, 2009); David Jackman, 'Preparing the Preacher,' in *When God's Voice Is Heard: Essays on Preaching*, ed. C. Green and David Jackman (Leicester: IVP, 1995), 175–187.

the overall flow of Jones' argument but he returns to his central point towards the end of the paper. He expresses concern that, while the conjunction of Word and Spirit is rightly stressed in contemporary treatments of preaching, insufficient attention is being given to the varying intensity and extensiveness of the Spirit's work as the Word is preached.[78] His point is similar to that of Eveson, Strivens and Olyott and, like his peers, he makes use of the sixteenth century debate as a backdrop to the contemporary discussion. But his view is rather more nuanced and he is careful to emphasise that Word and Spirit must never be disconnected. In this, he is arguably much closer to Calvin although we must defer our discussion of this until chapter four. Before we get to that, however, we will undertake a more detailed evaluation of the positions adopted by the radical Reformers, Luther, Zwingli and Bullinger.

78   Jones, 'Preaching the Word,' 86.

2

DEBATE AMONG THE REFORMERS

This chapter seeks to provide the crucial context for our lengthier discussion of Calvin's teaching on the relationship between Word and Spirit in preaching in chapter four. In the previous chapter, we saw that several commentators have sought to analyse contemporary views on Word and Spirit against the grid of the views held by the Protestant Reformers in the early sixteenth century. Stuart Olyott sounded the alarm against the resurgence of Martin Luther's error which has 'taken over vast sectors of British evangelicalism.'[1] Robert Strivens cautioned evangelicals against '[playing] down the independent role of the Spirit in the proclamation of the Word,' suggesting that they are aligning themselves with the Lutheran tradition.[2]

The early Reformers held a great diversity of views on the relationship between Word and Spirit in preaching. Although different schools of thought can be identified in a broad-brush

---

1 Olyott, 'Where Luther Got It Wrong,' 25.
2 Strivens, 'Preaching,' 71.

fashion, the reality is far more complex than is often portrayed. The different schools overlap at various points and there is an inevitable inter-mingling given the interaction of the main protagonists. Moreover, we must avoid the anachronistic error of reading back into the sixteenth century debate a later hardening of categories and allow the individuals to speak for themselves accepting whatever tensions their statements might present.

THE RADICALS

It is sensible to begin by considering the so-called 'radical Reformers' since the views of Martin Luther, Huldyrch Zwingli and Heinrich Bullinger are best understood against the backdrop of their interaction with the more radical wing of the Reformation. While Strivens focuses on Karlstadt and the Zwickau prophets, it is important to understand how these individuals are situated within the radical movement as a whole.

Classification of the Movement

Much ink has been spilt on classifying the third movement of the Reformation variously described as the 'left wing of the Reformation,'[3] or the radical Reformation.[4] Ernst Troeltsch divided it into two streams: the Spiritualists and the Anabaptists.[5] While the former rejected all external means of grace (preaching,

---

3   John T. McNeill, 'Left-Wing Religious Movements,' in *A Short History of Christianity*, ed. Archibald Gillies Baker (Chicago, IL: The University of Chicago Press, 1940), 127; Ronald H. Bainton, 'The Left Wing of the Reformation,' *Journal of Religion* 21, no. 2 (1941): 124.

4   Williams, *Spiritual and Anabaptist Writers*, 19–38; Walter Klassen, 'Spiritualization in the Reformation,' *The Mennonite Quarterly Review* 37 (1963): 67.

5   Ernst Troeltsch, *The Social Teaching of the Christian Churches*, trans. Olive Wyon, vol. 2 (Chicago, IL: University of Chicago Press, 1981), 2:691–770.

prayer, sacraments) as incompatible with the spiritual nature of Christianity, the latter enthusiastically embraced the external means but carefully distinguished their understanding of the means from those of the Magisterial Reformers (those Reformers who argued for the interdependence of the church and secular magistrate). Troeltsch's classification has the merit of simplicity and conceptual neatness but has attracted a significant degree of criticism for failing to recognise the deeply embedded mysticism present within Anabaptism.[6]

George Hunston Williams adopted a threefold classification. He distinguished between the Anabaptists and the Spiritualists on the basis of their fundamental orientation. The former 'looked steadily into the *past*' finding justification for their ecclesiology and doctrinal distinctives in the record of the early church. The Spiritualists, on the other hand, 'gazed mostly into the *future*' hoping for the re-establishment of the true church within their midst.[7] To these two camps Williams added the Evangelical Rationalists, a group that flourished in the Romance lands and emphasised 'the place of natural piety and of both intuitive and speculative reason alongside that of Scriptures.'[8] In common with the Anabaptists, the rationalists shared the desire to establish disciplined congregations along New Testament lines, but in common with the Spiritualists they exhibited a desire to reform theology which, in time, led to a systematic abandonment of orthodox doctrine.

Williams further sub-divided the Anabaptists and Spiritualists into three roughly corresponding streams.[9] Among the Anabaptists he distinguished between the evangelical (Swiss brethren, Obbenites), revolutionary (Münsterites) and contemplative

6   Klassen, 'Spiritualization in the Reformation,' 67–68.
7   Williams, *Spiritual and Anabaptist Writers*, 22–23.
8   Ibid., 23–24.
9   Ibid., 28.

(John Denck, Louis Haetzer) variants; and within the Spiritualists between the revolutionary (Zwickau prophets, Andreas Bodenestein von Karlstadt, Thomas Müntzer), rational (Sebastian Franck, Valentine Weigel) and evangelical (Caspar Schwenckfeld, Gabriel Ascherham) branches.[10]

While helpful, these classifications were inevitably over-rigid and liable to deceive.[11] Nevertheless, they serve our purpose to identify the key group of radical Reformers whom Luther engaged and opposed. They were the revolutionary spiritualists, men such as Müntzer and Karlstadt, for whom, as Williams puts it, 'the Spirit defined the Word, rather than the Eternal Word as recorded in Scripture (or tradition) defining and interpreting the Spirit.'

Luther's interactions with the Revolutionary Spiritualists

At first the revolutionary spiritualists were closely aligned with Luther as they rallied around him in his attack upon indulgences. Over time, however, the differences between them became apparent and the movement fragmented.

Thomas Müntzer

Thomas Müntzer is a great example of this. In his early years he shared many of Luther's views and it is arguable that Müntzer's decision to leave the monastery at Frohse in the autumn of 1518 was largely influenced by Luther's 95 theses. Nevertheless, Müntzer was also influenced by German mystical writings and Joachimite literature and this led to a serious disagreement with Luther over what Luther perceived to be Müntzer's politicisation

---

10   Ibid., 28–35.

11   See criticism of: Klassen, 'Spiritualization in the Reformation,' 68–69; Gordon Rupp, 'Word and Spirit in the First Years of the Reformation,' *Archiv für Reformationsgeschichte* 49 (1958): 15.

of his reforms.[12] Subsequently, Müntzer travelled around Germany, visiting Leipzig where he witnessed the debates between Karlstadt and Eck, and Luther and Eck. Eventually, he accepted a pastorate in Zwickau in May 1520 where he came under the influence of the conventicles (unofficial and unofficiated gatherings of lay people) which emphasised fresh outpourings of the Spirit in anticipation of an imminent return of Christ. As Troeltsch comments: 'His theology consisted of the mystical doctrine of passive deification, and the doctrine of the Holy Spirit, revealing His presence independently within the soul, merely stimulated and authenticated by the Word; this view he combined with Zwickau fanaticism.'[13]

Over time, Müntzer's social ideas became increasingly communistic, probably under the influence of Hussite and Taborite writings.[14] He also rejected infant baptism although he never fully embraced adult baptism.[15] In April 1521 he was expelled by the authorities from Zwickau and fled to Prague where he was initially welcomed with great enthusiasm. This support waned over time and he left Prague in December 1521, eventually settling in Allstedt where he became pastor in March 1523. There he was opposed by Luther, Frederick the Wise and George Spalatin and on 13 July 1524 he delivered his famous 'Sermon to the Princes.'

The sermon was delivered in Allstedt Castle before Duke John of Saxony (Frederick the Wise's brother), the Duke's son, and some of the Duke's officials and advisers. The Duke and his son had become divided over the role of the civil magistrate, the son siding with the more conservative views of Luther; while the Duke was more persuaded by the radical Reformers and their desire to see Mosaic Law imposed in evangelical territories.

---

12 Troeltsch, *Social Teaching*, 2:754; Williams, *Spiritual and Anabaptist Writers*, 32–33.

13 Troeltsch, *Social Teaching*, 2:754.

14 Ibid.

15 Williams, *Spiritual and Anabaptist Writers*, 32.

Müntzer chose Daniel 2 as his text, noting that Daniel was appointed adviser to the king because of his ability to interpret dreams. Müntzer acknowledged that there were many false prophets,[16] but insisted that he was a true prophet who the princes desperately needed to hear at a time such as this. He declared: 'Therefore a new Daniel must arise and interpret for you your vision and this [prophet], as Moses teaches (Deut 20:2), must go in front of the army. He must reconcile the anger of the princes and the enraged people.'[17] Müntzer applied Daniel's vision to his own day, insisting that they were living in the fifth kingdom (Dan. 2:41), pictured by feet of iron and clay, representing the mixing of princely and clerical power: 'The priests and all the wicked clerics are the vipers, as John the baptizer of Christ calls them (Matt. 3:7), and the temporal lords and princes are the eels, as is figuratively represented in Leviticus (11:10–12) by the fishes, etc.'[18] For Müntzer, the rock of Daniel 2:34 was Christ and his saints who were about to crush the fifth kingdom. [19]

Throughout the sermon, Müntzer railed against the 'debiblicising' of the office of magistrate which he thought was evident in the teaching of Luther and his colleagues. He spoke with passion, decrying the fact that the Lutheran clerics had 'made fools of' the princes 'so that everyone swears by the saints that the princes are in respect to their office a pagan people. They are said to be able to maintain nothing other than a civil unity.'[20] The social and ecclesiastical implications of the sermon are obvious but our focus is upon the claims that Müntzer made concerning the relationship between Word and Spirit in revelation. These claims were not peripheral to his argument because they buttressed Müntzer's broader agenda.

16   Ibid., 56–57.
17   Ibid., 64–65.
18   Ibid., 63.
19   Ibid., 63–64.
20   Ibid., 65.

Müntzer insisted with passion and vigour that God continues to reveal himself to his people in visions and audible words. He criticised those who denied immediate and direct revelation arguing that they were doing 'as the godless did to Jeremiah (20:7).'²¹ He called them 'unproven people' and likened them to 'the stiff-necked among the people of God who did not want to believe any prophet.'²² For Müntzer, occasional fresh revelation was consistent with the pattern of Scripture.²³ He recognised that there was a danger that such revelation might be corrupted by the devil or be the product of human improvisation and so cautioned that it should be 'tested in the Holy Bible.'²⁴ Nevertheless, for Müntzer, visions and revelation were essential for preachers, dukes and princes. In a thinly veiled attack on Luther and his followers, Müntzer declared:

> [W]hoever wishes, by reason of his fleshly judgment, to be utterly hostile about visions [and dreams] without any experience of them, rejecting them all, or [again, whoever] wishes to take them all in without distinction (because the false dream interpreters have done so much harm to the world through those who think only of their own renown or pleasure) – that surely [*either* extremist] will have a poor run of it and will hurl himself against the Holy Spirit [of these Last Days (Joel 2:28)]…It is true , and [I] know it to be true, that the Spirit of God is revealing to many elect, pious persons a decisive, inevitable, imminent reformation [accompanied] by great anguish, and it must be carried out to completion.²⁵

It is clear that Müntzer's social and ecclesiastical reforms were predicated on a separation of Word and Spirit in such a way that appeals for reform were based upon fresh outpourings of revelation rather than upon the written Word. For Müntzer, to

21   Ibid., 54.
22   Ibid., 55.
23   Ibid., 58.
24   Ibid., 60.
25   Ibid., 62.

deny dreams and visions was to oppose the Holy Spirit. Thus, Luther's opposition as recorded in his *Letter to the Princes*, related not only to his reforms but, more importantly, to the basis for them – his insistence that the Spirit provides new revelation directly and immediately through dreams and visions.

Shortly after his sermon, Müntzer and his colleagues were called before Duke John of Saxony at Weimar. The Duke issued an order for the closure of the printing press at Allstedt and shortly afterwards Müntzer fled to Mühlhausen where he became one of the leaders of the peasants' uprising. By this time, he had also rejected Luther's doctrine of salvation by faith alone and replaced it with a doctrine of the 'experienced cross' and the 'bitter Christ.'[26] On 15 May 1525, Müntzer led an army of 8,000 peasants in the Battle of Frankenhausen. The peasants were crushed and Müntzer was captured, tortured and beheaded.

Andreas Bodenestein von Karlstadt and the Zwickau Prophets

Like Müntzer, Andreas Bodenestein von Karlstdadt was initially closely aligned with Luther.[27] Both men had been profoundly influenced by their reading of the *Theologia Deutsch* and of Augustine's work,[28] but differences emerged over a number of important doctrinal issues. As Lohse has observed, Luther and Karlstadt adopted very different readings of Augustine's treatise *De Spiritu et Littera*. While Luther saw the treatise as supporting his view of God's righteousness and justification, Karlstadt focused upon Augustine's doctrine of the Spirit.[29] Lohse writes: '[Karlstadt] did not share Luther's accent on the 'imputation' of alien righteousness but stressed the gift of the Spirit as enabling

26   Ibid., 32–33.

27   Lohse, *Martin Luther's Theology*, 146–147.

28   Klassen, 'Spiritualization in the Reformation,' 73; Lohse, *Martin Luther's Theology*, 144–145.

29   See also: Rupp, 'Word and Spirit,' 19.

fulfilment of the law.'[30] This was the beginning of his strong dialectic between the Spirit and the Letter which stood in stark contrast to Luther's emphasis on Law and Gospel.[31] These doctrinal differences came to the fore during the debates with Eck at Leipzig, where Eck indicated that he was much closer to Karlstadt than Luther.[32] It also re-surfaced in disagreements concerning the epistle of James. Lohse comments: 'The divergence in their evaluation of James reflected differences not only in their understanding of Scripture but also in their view of justification and sanctification.'[33]

Against this backdrop, we must consider the events that took place at Wittenberg towards the end of 1521. Luther was in the Wartburg and spiritual leadership in Wittenberg had fallen to Karlstadt. At first Luther was very positive about the reforms taking place in the city under Karlstadt's leadership.[34] Writing to Spalatin on 5th December 1521, Luther commented: 'Everything else that I hear and see pleases me very much.'[35] This opinion had radically changed, however, by early 1522.[36] It seems that a combination of events contributed to this. Firstly, there was the impact of the Zwickau prophets who arrived in Wittenberg on 27 December 1521. They came intending to initiate reforms in the city and were well known for questioning the validity

30   Lohse, *Martin Luther's Theology*, 145.

31   Rupp, 'Word and Spirit,' 19.

32   Ulrich Bubenheimer, 'Karlstadt,' *Theologische Realenzyklopädie* 17 (1988): 650. Cited in: Lohse, *Martin Luther's Theology*, 145.

33   Lohse, *Martin Luther's Theology*, 145.

34   Ibid., 146–147.

35   Martin Luther, *Luther's Works Volume 48: Letters I*, ed. Helmut T. Lehmann and Gottfried G. Krodel (Philadelphia, PA: Fortress Press, 1963), 351(letter of Luther to Spalatin, 5 December 1521). Quoted in: Lohse, *Martin Luther's Theology*, 146.

36   Even in January 1522 Luther still gave his approval of Karlstadt's marriage despite the ban on priests marrying: Luther, *LW 48: Letters I*, 363(letter of Luther to Amsdorf, 13 January 1522).

of infant baptism.[37] Like Müntzer, however, their concerns extended well beyond ecclesiastical and sacramental issues and they were convinced that God spoke to them by means of visions and revelation. God was not limited to Scriptural revelation but could speak directly to his people and immediately. Luther repudiated this claim in the strongest of terms. While Karlstadt certainly was not one of the Zwickau prophets, it seems that the impact of the prophets on Wittenberg under Karlsdtadt's leadership shaped Luther's opinion of him.

Secondly, on Christmas Day 1521 Karlstadt performed the first Reformed communion service in Wittenberg. He did not wear vestments, refused to lift the host, and ensured that the cup was given to communicants. This was swiftly followed on 20 January 1522 by a decree of the imperial government, purporting to combat 'innovations against traditional Christian usage.'[38] The decree raised the real possibility that, should reforms continue apace, Wittenberg would lose the protection of the Duke of Saxony. Luther responded by appealing for order and insisting that, though the reforms may be right according to Scripture, they should not be implemented against the wishes of the authorities.[39]

The situation worsened still on 24 January 1522 when the Wittenberg City Council issued an order authorising the removal of images from the churches and affirming the reforms to the mass that Karlstadt had introduced on Christmas Day. As Lohse, comments: 'For Luther these detailed regulations surrendered evangelical freedom. They merely replaced the papal imposition of order with a no less strict Reformation order.'[40] It was not that he opposed the reforms but rather that he thought

---

37   Lohse, *Martin Luther's Theology*, 146.
38   Ibid., 147.
39   See Luther, *LW 51*, 73. Quoted in Lohse, *Martin Luther's Theology*, 147.
40   Lohse, *Martin Luther's Theology*, 147.

that the reforms should be brought about by convincing people's consciences through the teaching of the Word of God.

In March 1522, Luther returned to Wittenberg and preached a series of sermons in *Invocavit* week, attacking the Wittenberg reforms. This led to a serious fracturing of the relationship between Luther and Karlstadt, and in May 1523 Karlstadt accepted an invitation to pastor the church of Orlamünde. There he instituted his reforms in full, preaching on the right of ministers to marry, removing church art and music, rejecting infant baptism and denying the physical presence of Christ in the Lord's Supper. By early 1524, Luther had started to campaign against Karlstadt arguing that he should not preach or publish without Luther's consent. In his *Letter to the Princes*, sent in July, he argued that Müntzer and Karlstadt were in agreement. In September 1525, Karlstadt was exiled from Saxony by Frederick the Wise and Duke George of Saxony. After a brief period of internment he fled to Switzerland where he served as minister of the churches in Altstätten and Zürich, later settling in Basel where he died on 24 December 1541.

Commentators generally agree that the originality and mysticism of Karlstadt was more important than Müntzer's innovations but the former was largely overshadowed and assimilated with the boisterous tendencies of the latter.[41] Such assimilation is unfair since Karlstadt rejected Müntzer's invitation to join the League of the Elect and shunned the violence that led to the 1525 peasants' uprising. Moreover, he did not separate Word and Spirit in the same stark manner as Müntzer. His concern was not so much with the source of revelation and its implications for social reform as with the mystical distinction between Spirit and Letter. In rejecting Luther's emphasis upon justification by faith alone, he taught that sanctification 'was to be realized not merely on the bare authority of the Word of Scripture, but rather by

---

41   Rupp, 'Word and Spirit,' 18–19; Troeltsch, *Social Teaching*, 2:755.

the free inward movement of the Spirit which is merely aroused and controlled by the Scriptures.'[42] It was this emphasis upon the Spirit that led him to offer a spiritual critique of infant baptism and the physical presence of Christ in the Lord's Supper. It also stood behind many of his ecclesiological reforms. In this respect he had much in common with the Swiss Reformers which is why he found a home there in his later years. He was far more keen to unite Word and Spirit than Müntzer but, as Troeltsch notes, his 'essentially individualistic, irreconcilable form of mysticism… stood out in opposition to Luther's idea of a mediated salvation, bound up with an objective authority, which, for that reason, was capable of leading to an ecclesiastical organization.'[43]

The radical Reformation was a very diverse movement. Even within the narrower category of revolutionary spiritualists, there was diversity in the degree to which they separated Word and Spirit and the consequences of such a separation. It is now time to consider Luther's position and whether there is evidence for the claim that he radically changed his view in light of the teaching of the revolutionary spiritualists.

LUTHER

We begin with Luther's famous claim, 'the Word did it all'. Does this really provide evidence for Luther believing that the preached Word can yield results apart from the direct action of God?[44]

---

42   Troeltsch, *Social Teaching*, 2:755.

43   Ibid., 2:756.

44   Luther makes a similar comment in his lecture on Isaiah 55:10: 'So our building and promotion of the church is not the result of our works but the Word of God which we preach. He rails against the Enthusiasts, who despise the Word. Here you see that everything is produced by the Word' (Martin Luther, *Luther's Works Volume 17: Lectures on Isaiah 40-66*, ed. Jaroslav Pelikan and Hilton C. Oswald [Saint Louis, MO: Concordia Publishing House, 1972], 257–258).

The Second Invocavit Sermon

In Olyott's reproduction of the quotation he gives the impression that the statement was made towards the end of Luther's life when he was looking back 'on all that had happened' during the Reformation. In fact, the quotation comes from the second of eight sermons preached by Luther during the *Invocavit* week of 1522. As we have seen, these sermons were preached by Luther to address the Roman Mass and the appropriate Protestant response to it in light of the actions taken by Karlstadt and the Zwickau prophets earlier in the year.[45] Thus it is an early work and does not directly address the relationship between Word and Spirit. Instead Luther's insistence that the 'Word did everything' was directed against those who might be tempted to follow the radical Reformers in seeking to abolish the Mass 'by force.' It had nothing to do with the radical Reformers' view on the relationship between Word and Spirit. A little earlier in the sermon, Luther insisted that 'no one should be dragged away from [the Mass] by the hair; for it should be left to God, and his Word should be allowed to work alone, without our work or interference.'[46] Luther's emphasis is upon the Word working apart from our works, not apart from God's work. What follows is so important that it bears quotation in full:

> Why? Because it is not in my power or hand to fashion the hearts of men as the potter molds the clay and fashion them at my pleasure [Ecclus. 33:13]. I can get no further than their ears; their hearts I cannot reach. And since I cannot pour faith into their hearts, I cannot, nor should I, force any one to have faith. That is God's work alone, who causes faith to live in the heart. Therefore we should give free course to the Word and not add our works to it. We have the *jus verbi* [right to speak] but not the *executio* [power to

---

45 See the editor's introduction to the sermons in: Luther, *LW 51*, 69–70.
46 Ibid., 76.

accomplish]. We should preach the Word, but the results must be left solely to God's good pleasure.[47]

Far from claiming that the preached Word yields results apart from God's direct action, Luther is making precisely the opposite claim. It is God's work, not the preacher's (no matter how careful he is in his exegesis), to cause faith to live in the heart. The preacher's role is to preach the Word and the results must be 'left solely to God's good pleasure.' If people fail to respond, Luther 'simply allowed the Word to act and prayed for them.'[48] These words could have come from Olyott's own mouth. The famous 'the Word did it all' claim, when understood in its original context, does not in any way support Olyott's representation of Luther's views. Whether support can be found in a broader survey of Luther's work is a different question.

The impact of the Wittenberg Reformers on Luther's thought

Roberts Strivens and Bernard Lohse both argue that Luther's conflict with the Wittenberg reformers had a profound effect upon his understanding of the relationship between Word and Spirit in preaching.[49] They compare his exposition of the *Magnificat* sent to Prince John Frederick, Duke of Saxony, on 10th March 1521 with his later treatise *Against the Heavenly Prophets* in 1525. Luther began the former as follows: 'No one can correctly understand God or His Word unless he has received such understanding immediately from the Holy Spirit. But no one can receive it from the Holy Spirit without experiencing, proving and feeling it. In such experience the Holy Spirit instructs us as in His own school, outside of which nothing is learned but empty

47   Ibid.
48   Ibid., 77.
49   Strivens, 'Preaching,' 60–61; Lohse, *Martin Luther's Theology*, 148.

words and prattle.'[50] Strivens describes these as words with which we can all identify, emphasising the necessity of the Spirit's work if preaching is to be of spiritual benefit to us.[51] He contrasts this with Luther's discussion of the relationship between Word and Spirit in *Against the Heavenly Prophets*:

> Now when God sends forth his holy gospel he deals with us in a twofold manner, first outwardly, then inwardly. Outwardly he deals with us through the oral word of the gospel and through material signs, that is, baptism and the sacrament of the altar. Inwardly, he deals with us through the Holy Spirit, faith and other gifts. But whatever their measure or order, the outward factors should and must precede.[52]

Strivens argues that Luther ties together the Spirit and the means of grace much more closely here, insisting that the Word must come first and implying 'that the one cannot work without the other.'[53] In a similar vein, Lohse describes Luther as teaching that '[t]he Spirit does not work independently of the external Word but always in union with it.'[54]

Context is crucial and should not be overlooked. Luther's comments on the *Magnificat* were addressed to a young prince who had pledged his support for Luther following the papal bull of 15th June 1520. It is a pastoral sermon in which Luther counsels the young prince about how he should live and rule. Mary's example as one who was lowly but lifted to extraordinary heights and yet still magnified God is held out as an example. In his accompanying letter, Luther writes:

50   Martin Luther, *Luther's Works Volume 21: The Sermon on the Mount (sermons) and the Magnificat*, ed. Jaroslav Pelikan (Philadelphia, PA: Fortress Press, 1956), 299.

51   Strivens, 'Preaching,' 60.

52   Martin Luther, *Luther's Works Volume 40: Church and Ministry II*, ed. Conrad Bergendoff (Philadelphia, PA: Fortress Press, 1958), 146.

53   Strivens, 'Preaching,' 61.

54   Lohse, *Martin Luther's Theology*, 148.

Now, in all of Scripture I do not know anything that serves such a purpose so well as this sacred hymn of the most blessed Mother of God, which ought indeed to be learned and kept in mind by all who would rule well and be helpful lords. In it she really sings sweetly about the fear of God, what sort of Lord He is, and especially what His dealings are with those of low and high degree.[55]

This is the situational context of Luther's emphasis upon the experiential primacy of the Holy Spirit in the right understanding of Scripture. More important still is the redemptive historical context of his remarks. Luther is commenting on the response of praise of Mary, the mother of Jesus, *theotokos* as the Eastern fathers insisted.[56] And his point, as he opens the sermon, is that Mary's song of praise is spoken at this seminal point in redemptive history out of her own experience, in which she was enlightened and instructed by the Spirit.[57] There is something unique about her experience and it should not to be taken as normative for the Christian life. Therefore Luther's comments ought to be strictly confined. Even where he develops the point further discussing creation *ex nihilo*, his point is that 'out of that which is nothing, worthless, despised, wretched and dead, [God] makes that which is something precious, honourable blessed and living.'[58] He is not making any general statement about the relationship between Word and Spirit in preaching. The focus throughout is upon Mary as a speaker of Spirit-inspired words rather than Mary as a hearer of the Word.

Likewise the context of *Against the Heavenly Prophets* is fundamental to understanding the significance of the words quoted by Lohse and Strivens and what Luther intended to teach

---

55   Luther, *LW 21: Sermon on the Mount and Magnificat*, 298.

56   Richard A. Norris, ed., *The Christological Controversy* (Philadelphia, PA: Fortress Press, 1980), 132–134.

57   Luther, *LW 21: Sermon on the Mount and Magnificat*, 299–300.

58   Ibid., 299.

when he claimed that 'outward factors should and must precede.'[59] He was opposing Karlstadt, who Luther claims 'subordinate[d] God's outward order to an inner spiritual one.' Karlstadt had been arguing that God should be found without means, urging believers not to go to the 'outward gospel' contained in the written Word but instead to 'remain in "self-abstraction"' where '[a] heavenly voice will come, and God himself will speak to you.'[60] Luther rightly recognised that this tore the very gospel away from people by suggesting that they could come to God rather than that God had come to them. Luther continues:

> Do you not see here the devil, the enemy of God's order? With all his mouthing of the words, 'Spirit, Spirit, Spirit,' [Karlstadt] tears down the bridge, the path, the way, the ladder, and all the means by which the Spirit might come to you. Instead of the outward order of God in the material sign of baptism and the oral proclamation of the Word of God he wants to teach you, not how the Spirit comes to you but how you come to the Spirit.[61]

This is highly significant. Olyott and Strivens appear to be concerned that, by uniting Word and Spirit, Luther undermined divine monergism. As Strivens so provocatively put it in the title to his paper, Luther's position appears to teach that preaching is efficacious *ex opere operato*. But far from undermining divine monergism, Luther's primary concern in emphasising the order of Word and Spirit, was to *defend* it. God comes to the believer, not the other way round. And he does so through means.

Luther's emphasis upon 'order' must be read in the context of his broader concerns about the practice of the revolutionary spiritualists.[62] Not only were they reducing the external Word to

---

59   Luther, *LW 40: Church and Ministry II*, 146.

60   Ibid., 147.

61   Ibid.

62   Luther emphasised the importance of order elsewhere. See for example: Martin Luther, *Martin Luther's Tabletalk: Luther's Comments on Life, the Church and the Bible.*, ed. William Hazlitt [Fearn: Christian Heritage, 2003], 192.

an inner voice, but also, in Luther's opinion, they were turning spiritual things, such as the Lord's Supper, into human works. Luther writes: 'That which God has made a matter of inward faith and spirit they convert into a human work. But what God has ordained as an outward word and sign and work they convert into an inner spirit. They place the mortification of the flesh prior to faith, even prior to the Word.'[63] It is for this reason that Luther is so concerned about order. Mortification and vivification cannot happen before someone has received Christ though faith and such receiving of Christ cannot happen without hearing the gospel. To argue otherwise, in Luther's thinking, is to substitute human works for the gospel. Luther concludes his argument with words that bear quotation in full:

> Before all other works and acts you hear the Word of God, through which the Spirit convinces the world of its sin (John 16:8). When we acknowledge our sin, we hear of the grace of Christ. In this Word the Spirit comes and gives faith where and to whom he wills. Then you proceed to the mortification and the cross and the works of love. Whoever wants to propose to you another order, you can be sure, is of the devil. Such is the spirit of this Karlstadt.[64]

Luther is clear that the Spirit is free and comes to give faith to whomsoever he wills. There is not a hint of the Word functioning *ex opere operato* here. As Regin Prenter writes, commenting on this passage: 'The Spirit is not dependent upon the Word, but retains his sovereignty over the Word…the polemic against the enthusiasts does not make Luther ignore the thought about the sovereignty of the Spirit and the insufficiency of the outward Word.'[65] Even the close functional union of Word and Spirit which both Lohse and Strivens comment upon must be read

---

63   Luther, *LW 40: Church and Ministry II*, 148–149.

64   Ibid., 149.

65   Regin Prenter, *Spiritus Creator*, trans. John M. Jensen (Philadelphia, PA: Fortress Press, 1953), 250.

in the context of Luther's broader concerns, and it cannot be assumed on the basis of these texts alone that Luther moved to a position where the Spirit could never work independently of the Word. A broader survey of Luther's work is required and it is to this that we now turn.

A Broader survey of Luther's Work

Space prohibits an exhaustive survey and so we will instead focus upon the work of two eminent Luther scholars, Regin Prenter and Paul Althaus.

Regin Prenter

Prenter begins his chapter on the means used by the Holy Spirit by acknowledging that, for Luther, the Word is unambiguously the means of the Holy Spirit.[66] This, however, raises the larger question concerning the nature of the relationship between Word and Spirit. Are they so connected that the Spirit is always present whenever the Word is preached? Or can they work apart from each other?

Prenter identifies two streams of thought in Luther. Firstly, the Reformer carried his law-gospel dichotomy into his attitude towards Scripture, adopting Augustine's distinction between the outward and the inward Word.[67] Relying upon 1 Corinthians 3:7, Luther insists, '[t]he outward Word is only the means which God uses when he writes his own living Word into the heart,' and he does that by the Spirit.[68] Prenter summarises this stream of thought as teaching that the outward Word 'becomes a mere symbol, a signpost which directs us to the point where the Spirit

66   Ibid., 101.
67   See also for a detailed evaluation of the role of letter and Spirit in Luther: Gerhard Ebeling, *Luther: An Introduction to His Thought*, trans. R. A. Wilson (Philadelphia, PA: Fortress Press, 1970), 93–109.
68   Prenter, *Spiritus Creator*, 102.

is, but does not mediate the Spirit.'[69] Word and Spirit are distinct and it is the Spirit alone which brings efficacy to the Word.

This stream of thought must be compared with statements that appear to point in the opposite direction. Luther insisted 'that the Word is the instrument of the Spirit, that the outward Word is the incarnation of the Spirit, and it corresponds to the Spirit as the voice corresponds to man's breathing, or as rays of the sun correspond to the warmth of the sun.'[70] These descriptions and similes clearly imply an incredibly close relationship between Word and Spirit, even implying that the outward Word necessarily and always brings the Spirit with it. It almost seems as if the Spirit is 'a mere attribute of the Word.'[71]

How are these contrasting statements to be reconciled? Prenter considers the claim that the tension can be resolved by supposing a development in Luther's thought. This, of course, is the argument advanced by Strivens and Rupp in their contrast between Luther's work before and after Karlstadt's reforms. Prenter acknowledges that there is some evidence for such a development but claims that it is only partial.[72] A closer examination reveals that the instrumental view of the Word is clearly present in Luther's earlier writings such as in his first lecture on the Psalms, and his emphasis upon the sovereignty of the Spirit; and the insufficiency of the outward Word does not subside once he comes into conflict with the revolutionary spiritualists. Prenter concludes:

> We are not therefore to understand that the struggle with the enthusiasts has caused a change in Luther's view on this point. The view of the relationship between the Spirit and the Word which Luther later used against the enthusiasts was fully formed before

69   Ibid., 103.

70   Ibid., 103. See also: Dennis Ngien, 'Theology of Preaching in Martin Luther,' *Themelios* 28 (2003): 43.

71   Prenter, *Spiritus Creator*, 104.

72   Ibid.

that struggle. The struggle only developed a more polemic keenness in the formulation of the expressions but no real change.[73]

Prenter seeks to resolve the tension, which he insists is present throughout Luther's work, by positing that the Word of God for Luther was only Christ himself, not the written Word.[74] This is a controversial claim and part of Prenter's larger thesis, but it need not detain us here. What is significant for our purposes is that the tension between the sovereignty of the Spirit and the instrumentality of the Word continues throughout Luther's work and cannot be resolved simply by reference to a presumed development of Luther's thought following his interactions with the revolutionary spiritualists.

One point upon which Prenter is especially helpful is in showing the sacramental quality of the Word in Luther's thought. This explains why the Spirit cannot work without the outward Word. The Word is God's means of presenting Christ to us. Prenter writes: 'The outward Word can and shall be the means of God's sacramental message to man, while the absence of the outward Word leaves the man alone with himself and his own recollections and ideas.'[75] This is why the Word is the instrumental means of the Spirit – because it presents Christ to believers. The sacramental quality of the Word was important to the sixteenth century Reformers and is a point to which we will return in our consideration of Calvin.

Returning to the question of whether Luther thought that Word and Spirit can work apart from each other, Prenter suggests

73   Ibid., 105.

74   Ibid., 106–112. Luther clearly used Word in both senses, see: Martin Luther, *Luther's Works Volume 54: Table Talk*, ed. Theodore Gerhardt Tappert (Philadelphia, PA: Fortress Press, 1967), 395.

75   Prenter, *Spiritus Creator*, 113. Prenter expands upon this later in the book when he describes the Word as a sacrament because it is not merely the bearer of abstract content but rather the 'bearer of God's concrete act of revelation' (Ibid., 137).

that they can, but in a carefully qualified way. Firstly, the Word
may work without the Spirit in the sense that it may be preached
and received as just a letter. 'As a letter the Word is law and not
gospel.'[76] In other words, the Word can be preached without the
accompanying presence of the Spirit of blessing. Likewise, it is
possible for the Spirit to be present without the Word because
the Spirit has his own existence in God's glory and is not bound
either to the Word or to us. But, and here is an important
qualification, 'as the revealing Spirit, as the Spirit which is come
to us, he cannot be without the Word.'[77]

According to Prenter, a tension runs throughout Luther's work
and it is reductionist to seek to explain it away as a perceived
development in Luther's thinking. The Spirit is sovereign and
works where and when he likes. This is taught even in Luther's
later works such as *Against the Heavenly Prophets* where he insisted
that the Spirit 'comes and gives faith where and to whom he
wills.'[78] At the same time, the Spirit has bound himself to outward
means in relation to his revelatory function: 'As the instrument
of the Spirit the Word is therefore always the proclaiming Word,
a contemporary and sacramental Word, which gives Christ as
a gift, and in which he is the acting subject.'[79] Strivens is right
to claim that 'the means of grace were…essential in Luther's
thinking' and Rupp is correct that 'for Luther, Word and Spirit
were not to be parted asunder.'[80] But that does not imply that
the Word functions *ex opere operato* or that the Spirit is somehow
limited in his freedom to determine whom he blesses in the
hearing of the Word.

---

76   Prenter, *Spiritus Creator*, 122.
77   Ibid.
78   Luther, *LW 40: Church and Ministry II*, 149.
79   Prenter, *Spiritus Creator*, 123.
80   Strivens, 'Preaching,' 62; Rupp, 'Word and Spirit,' 25.

Paul Althaus

Althaus presents a broadly similar assessment of Luther's thought suggesting that his understanding of the relationship between Word and Spirit can be summarised in two sentences: '(1) The Spirit does not speak without the word. (2) The Spirit speaks through and in the word.'[81] Luther acknowledged that God could have chosen to work in men without using the Word but he had decided not to: 'It has pleased God not to give us the Spirit without the Word but through the Word that he might have us as workers together with him, we sounding forth without what he alone breathes within wheresoever he will.'[82] Althaus notes that this argument was advanced in particular against the enthusiasts in response to their claims to have received extra-biblical revelation. As well as being the means used by God to work in people the Word is also spiritually powerful in itself: 'The Spirit does not work alone without the word but rather in and through the word.'[83] For Luther, the authentication of the Word can be described as both 'the self-testimony of the word and the testimony of the Holy Spirit.'[84] This underlines the indissoluble unity of Word and Spirit and, like Prenter, Althaus sees this reinforced by Luther's use of human speech to illustrate the relationship: 'One cannot separate the voice from the breath. Whoever refuses to hear the voice gets nothing out of the breath either.'[85]

Having recognised the unity of Word and Spirit in Luther, Althaus proceeds to consider the question of whether the Spirit

81 Paul Althaus, *The Theology of Martin Luther*, trans. Robert C. Schultz (Philadelphia, PA: Fortress Press, 1966), 36.

82 WA 18, 695. Cited in: Ibid., 36, fn. 7.

83 Citing WA 9, 632f (Ibid., 37).

84 Althaus, *Luther*, 38. See also: Martin Luther, *Luther's Works Volume 29: Lectures on Titus, Philemon, and Hebrews*, ed. Jaroslav Pelikan and Walter A. Hansen (Saint Louis, MO: Concordia Publishing House, 1968), 164; Luther, *Luther's Works Volume 54: Table Talk*, 318.

85 WA 9, 633. Cited in: Althaus, *Luther*, 38.

always accompanies the Word. Althaus is careful to present a balanced and qualified answer here. He distinguishes the Word and Spirit in Luther's thought to emphasise that the Word does not overwhelm the heart as a result of 'an inherent dynamic which the word possesses in itself.' Althaus continues: 'On the contrary the activity of the Spirit which always occurs through the word, must first be added to the preaching and hearing of the external word; and it is not always added at once.'[86] So the power of the Spirit is not delegated to the Word in Luther's thought, but rather works freely through it. Althaus insists that Luther did not consider preaching to be effective *ex opere operato*.[87] He writes: '[God] does not give the preacher control over his Spirit. Sometimes the preaching and the hearing must wait for him. We have to pray for the gift of the Spirit to accompany the word.'[88] Luther himself writes: 'God wills that we should teach the law. When we have done this he himself shall see who will be converted by it.'[89] God decides who to make the Word effective for and he also choses when to make it effective.[90] Sometimes this may happen many years after the external word was received: 'Comfort does not come to us without the word, which the Holy Spirit effectively calls to mind and enkindles in our hearts, even though it has not been heard for ten years.'[91] So God is sovereign and free in deciding the 'when' and 'on whom' of the effectiveness of his Word but this 'in no way changes the fact that the Spirit

---

86   Althaus, *Luther*, 38.

87   Elsewhere Luther insists that 'it is not enough to possess the revelation of the Word: it is also necessary to have the enlightenment of the Holy Spirit so as to know its meaning.' (Martin Luther, *Luther's Works Volume 24: Sermons on the Gospel of St. John*, ed. Jaroslav Jan Pelikan and Daniel E. Poellot [Saint Louis, MO: Concordia Publishing House, 1957], 367); Cited in: Wood, *Captive to the Word*, 160.

88   Althaus, *Luther*, 39.

89   WA 39, I, 369. Cited in: Ibid., 39, fn. 17.

90   See also Luther, *Tabletalk*, 192.

91   Martin Luther, *Luther's Works Volume 14: Selected Psalms 3*, ed. Jaroslav Pelikan (Philadelphia, PA: Fortress Press, 1958), 62.

is bound to the word.' He speaks directly to the heart by the external word and by the external word alone. Thus, according to Althaus, while insisting that Word and Spirit are inextricably tied, Luther also acknowledged that the Spirit is free to work when and on whom He wishes through the Word.

On the issue of means, Althaus deconstructs a popular parody arguing that Luther recognised the immediate work of the Spirit and the enthusiasts taught that the Spirit works through means. The difference according to Althaus lies in the fact that they see this taking place at different times and in different ways. He continues: 'The enthusiasts teach and practice methods of preparing oneself to receive the Spirit. Luther rejects such a technique of treating souls…There is only one true preparation; and that is to preach, to hear, and to read the word.'[92] As we observed in our discussion of *Against the Heavenly Prophets*, the conflict between Luther and the revolutionary spiritualists (enthusiasts) turned upon whether the movement in salvation was from God to man or the other way round. In other words, it concerned the doctrine of justification. The revolutionary spiritualists' teaching upon preparation led to a man-centred soteriology and their rejection of means in revelation led to doctrinal convictions that had drifted a long way from scriptural moorings. Althaus describes it extremely well:

> The enthusiasts teach a working of God through means, that is, human preparation, precisely at the point at which it dare not be asserted because it limits the freedom of God. And these enthusiasts teach that God works without means precisely at the point where God has made the Christian dependent on the means of grace. Luther rejects the spiritualists' position on both points because of his understanding of justification. Luther preserves both the fact that God has bound himself to the word and the fact that he remains free.[93]

92   Althaus, *Luther*, 41.
93   Ibid.

Summary

Our brief review of Luther's work has shown that the fact that Luther united Word and Spirit together did not mean that he failed to distinguish between them. He was sensitive to the need to emphasise the primacy of the Word against both the church in Rome and the revolutionary spiritualists. In *The Babylonian Captivity of the Church*, Luther wrote: 'It is plain therefore, that the beginning of our salvation is a faith which clings to the Word of the promising God, who, without any effort on our part, in free and unmerited mercy takes the initiative and offers us the word of his promise.'[94] For Luther, the primacy of the Word was bound up with the doctrine of salvation by grace alone. God deals with us through His word of promise and we deal with him through faith in that same word.[95] But that does not imply that preaching is effective *ex opere operato* or that the operation of the Spirit is indistinguishable from that of the Word. Even when Luther exclaimed 'The Word, I say, and only the Word is the vehicle of God's grace'[96] he was speaking of the Word in contrast to the sacraments rather than to the Spirit.[97] For Luther '[w]hile preaching is indispensable to the engendering of faith, it is the work of the Holy Spirit to give faith in the heart.'[98] The office of the Holy Spirit is to teach and bring home God's Word.[99] Thus,

94   Martin Luther, *Luther's Works Volume 36: Word and Sacrament II*, ed. Abdel Ross Wentz, trans. A. T. W. Steinhauser (Philadelphia, PA: Fortress Press, 1959), 39.

95   Luther, *LW 36*, 42.

96   Luther, In epistolam S. Pauli ad Galatas commentarius (1519), on Gal. 3:2, WA 2:509. Locher cites this as evidence for a conflation of Word and Spirit (Gottfried Wilhelm Locher, *Zwingli's Thought: New Perspectives* [Leiden: E. J. Brill, 1981], 286).

97   See Gerrish's helpful discussion where he suggests that the key lies in what Luther discovered to be the sacramentality of the preached word (Brian Albert Gerrish, *Thinking with the Church: Essays in Historical Theology* [Grand Rapids, MI: Eerdmans, 2010], 272–273).

98   Ngien, 'Preaching in Martin Luther,' 43.

99   WA 57.185.21. Cited in: Rupp, *The Righteousness of God*, 210. See also Wood, *Captive to the Word*, 160–161.

while the preaching of the Word is the duty of man it is only God by his Spirit who can put the Word into a person's heart.[100]

There is no evidence for the view that Luther believed the efficacy of preaching to reside in human power or technique. Nor are there grounds for believing that Luther held that preaching was effective by its very act. He had a high view of Scripture, asking 'who will not be turned back and will not fall and perish whose conscience rebuked by the Word of God, gives a condemning sentence against himself?'[101] At the same time, however, he recognised that the Word in itself would not convert anyone. It is the Spirit who writes the Word upon people's hearts.

Luther's thinking upon the relationship between Word and Spirit was forged in the midst of his conflict with the revolutionary spiritualists. There does, however, appear to be harmony between his pre-1521 views and those articulated after the Wittenberg reforms. Throughout his writing he emphasised both the unity of Word and Spirit (with an emphasis upon the Word being the instrumental means of the Spirit) and the distinction between Word and Spirit (consistent with the law-gospel dichotomy). He never resolved this tension although, due to the polemical context in which much of his writing was produced, unity was often emphasised to the detriment of distinction. Perhaps this is why later Lutheranism headed off in the direction which Strivens highlights, but in emphasising the unity of Word and Spirit, Luther never went so far as to conflate them or to suggest that the power of the Spirit had been delegated to the Word. He was clear that Word and Spirit remain distinct and that the Spirit is necessary to teach and bring home the Word.

---

100   WA 10, III, 260. Cited in: Althaus, *Luther*, 39. See also WA 57.186.25 cited in: Rupp, *The Righteousness of God*, 210; Luther, *Tabletalk*, 107; Philip S. Watson, *Let God Be God: An Interpretation of the Theology of Martin Luther* (London: Epworth Press, 1947), 167.

101   WA 5.294.21, cited in: Rupp, *The Righteousness of God*, 233.

THE SWISS REFORMERS

Although it is sometimes overlooked in discussions of Zwingli's theology, the Swiss Reformer maintained a very high view of Scripture.

A High View of Scripture

Zwingli was convinced that the Word of God has the power to change the world. In his early work, *The Clarity and Certainty of the Word of God*, he wrote that 'the whole course of nature must be altered rather than that the Word of God should not remain and be fulfilled.'[102] God's Word can 'never be undone or destroyed or resisted' Zwingli insisted, and God will never leave it powerless.[103] In words highly reminiscent of Luther's 'the Word did it all,' Zwingli wrote: 'Truly the Word of God will take its course as surely as the Rhine; you can dam it up for a while, but you cannot stop its flow.'[104] We should be left in no doubt that Zwingli had a high view of Scripture.

Interactions with the Radicals

Zwingli carried this high view of Scripture into his debates with the radical Reformers. He accused them of subordinating Scripture to their own spirits whenever it suited them: 'For as often as by the use of scripture they are driven to the point of having to say, I yield, straightaway they talk about 'the Spirit' and deny Scripture. As if indeed the heavenly Spirit were ignorant of

---

102   Geoffrey William Bromiley, *Zwingli and Bullinger* (Philadelphia, PA: Westminster Press, 1963), 70.

103   Ibid., 72.

104   Z III 488. Cited in: Locher, *Zwingli's Thought*, 71.

the sense of scripture which is written under his guidance or were anywhere inconsistent with himself.'[105]

In opposing the radicals, he cited Jesus' own example of appealing to Scripture even though his miracles and teaching were sufficient testimony to his speaking from God.[106] He even pleaded the supremacy of Scripture against Luther declaring in his *Two Replies to Luther's Book* that 'no one should boast of the freedom of the Spirit who teaches or acts against God's word.'[107] For Zwingli, Luther had become like one of the radical Reformers by adopting positions he could not defend from Scripture.

This strong emphasis upon the Word must be balanced against Zwingli's spiritualist tendencies which aligned him much more closely with the radical Reformers especially concerning the sacraments.[108] Just as Zwingli associated Luther with Rome in his sacramentology, so Luther associated Zwingli with Karlstadt and the radical Reformers.[109] Indeed, it was not until the Marburg Colloquy in 1529 that Luther began to more carefully distinguish Zwingli from the radicals Reformers.[110] Underlying their differences were contrasting views about the Spirit and the use of means. This inevitably flowed over into Zwingli's understanding of the relationship between Word and Spirit in preaching.

Word and Spirit

It is this, and the legacy it left in Zurich, that Luther reputedly attacked in his comments recorded in Tabletalk:

---

105   Cited in: W. P Stephens, *The Theology of Huldrych Zwingli.*, New ed. (Oxford: Clarendon, 1988), 132.

106   Ibid.

107   Ibid., 133.

108   Klassen, 'Spiritualization in the Reformation,' 74.

109   Stephens, *Theology of Zwingli*, 47.

110   Locher, *Zwingli's Thought*, 284.

[Bullinger] is confused and does not know what he thinks and believes. I indeed see their fallacies and deception; they do not want it to appear that they have erred. Both sides, we and they, stand on two extreme positions between which there is no middle ground, nor can be. They absolutely reject the spoken word and efficacy of the sacraments; we, however, insist strongly on them…[They] separated Word and Spirit, excluded from God, who was working there, the man who preached and taught the Word…and thought the Holy Spirit should be given and would work without the Word.[111]

In typically polemical fashion, Luther describes their differences in stark and perhaps over-stated terms. It is undeniable though that Zwingli and his successors held a different conception of Word and Spirit to that of Luther. Although Zwingli emphasised the unity of Word and Spirit, the Spirit being the author and interpreter of Scripture,[112] he repeatedly placed his emphasis upon the Spirit. This is seen, in part, in the reversal of the order of Word and Spirit that we saw in Luther. For Zwingli the order is usually (although not always) Spirit and Word. In response to his Roman opponents, he wrote:

Before I say anything or listen to the teaching of man, I will first consult the mind of the Spirit of God (Psalm 85): 'I will hear what God the Lord will speak.' Then you should reverently ask God for his grace, that he may give you his mind and Spirit, so that you will not lay hold of your opinion but of his. And have a firm trust that he will teach you a right understanding, for all wisdom is of God the Lord. And then go to the written word of the gospel…You must be *theodidacti*, that is, taught of God, not men: that is what the Truth itself said (John 6) and it cannot lie.[113]

Sometimes too much weight has been placed upon this reversal of order. Zwingli's point was simply that the Word cannot be

---

111   Tischreden, Martin Luther's sammtliche Werke (Erlangen) 57: 36–37. Cited in: Klassen, 'Spiritualization in the Reformation,' 72.

112   Z XIV 181.11–18. Cited in: Stephens, *Theology of Zwingli*, 132.

113   Z I 377.7–21. Cited in: Ibid., 60.

understood through human understanding alone but only through the illuminating power of the Holy Spirit.[114] As we have seen, Luther wholeheartedly affirmed this.[115] Likewise, the rationale behind Luther's order—that the Spirit speaks through the Scriptures (over and against the claims of the radicals)—was affirmed by Zwingli. But there did exist a discernible and important difference of emphasis between the two Reformers. Gottfried Locher has described it well: 'To the end of his days Martin Luther marvelled that the Spirit should bind himself to the Word. In much the same way, Zwingli guarded most passionately the truth that the Word is bound to the Spirit.'[116] Zwingli insisted that the Spirit was not bound to means and indeed was free of means. He wrote: 'Neither guidance nor vehicle is necessary for the Spirit; He himself is the power and vehicle by which everything is carried along.'[117] It is statements such as this that led Luther to accuse Zwingli and his followers of separating Word and Spirit. But what led Zwingli to such a separation?

One of his primary reasons for emphasising the Spirit was a concern to show the internal perspicuity of Scripture over and against Rome's claim to be the authoritative interpreter of the Word. In *The Clarity and Certainty of the Word of God*, Zwingli wrote: 'once God has taught us with this anointing, that is, his Spirit, we do not need any other teacher, for there is no more error, but only the pure truth in which we are to abide.'[118] By emphasising the Spirit as the sole interpreter of Scripture, Zwingli sought to free believers from dependence upon the church in

---

114   See Bromiley, *Zwingli and Bullinger*, 36.

115   See for example WA 10, III, 260. Cited in: Althaus, *Luther*, 39.

116   Locher, *Zwingli's Thought*, 13.

117   S IV 10. Cited in: Ibid., 12.

118   'The Clarity and Certainty of the Word of God' in Bromiley, *Zwingli and Bullinger*, 82–83.

Rome and to prevent them from replacing one external authority with another.[119]

Secondly, Zwingli's emphasis upon the sovereign freedom of God contributed to his tendency to separate Word and Spirit and to deprecate means. As Stephens notes, '[s]uch a theology can give no independent power to anyone or anything apart from God.'[120] Of course, such concerns impacted Zwingli's sacramentology as well, but we shall defer our discussion of that until the next chapter. For now, we simply note that Zwingli's emphasis upon the sovereign freedom of the Spirit led to some of the more unorthodox aspects of his theology such as his belief that pious unbelievers (such as Socrates and Seneca) would be saved because of their obedience to occasional special communications from the Holy Spirit. Zwingli wrote: 'Thus the heathen did not know the law of nature by virtue of their own reasoning but by the illuminating Spirit of God, even though he was not known to them...Since they did not have faith, but did understand the law of nature, this must have come from God alone...'[121] As Klassen notes: 'Here Zwingli clearly accepts a free and unmediated influence of God's Spirit' unbounded by the Word.[122]

Thirdly, Zwingli's determination to maintain a robust distinction between Word and Spirit is in part explicable by what he saw to lie at the heart of the Reformation. For Zwingli, the enemy of faith was idolatry and all man-made traditions. He was determined that the traditions of the mass ought not to be replaced by another external work—preaching. As Locher explains, Zwingli conceived of two alternatives: 'either the Word of God spoken into our heart by the Spirit of God himself—or the word of

---

119   Ibid., 55.

120   Stephens, *Theology of Zwingli*, 135.

121   Z II 327. Cited in: Locher, *Zwingli's Thought*, 179. See also: Bromiley, *Zwingli and Bullinger*, 33.

122   Klassen, 'Spiritualization in the Reformation,' 75–76.

man, whether this word of man comes in the form of divine service, official activity, ceremony, sacrament or—preaching.'[123]

Such concerns led to a separation of Word and Spirit in Zwingli's thinking. Stephens is right when he suggests that Zwingli's understanding of the relationship of the Spirit and the Word was not 'precisely formulated'. [124] Tensions exist throughout and while he sometimes emphasised the unity of Word and Spirit, at other times he distinguished them to the point of separation in the interests of maintaining the freedom of the Spirit. As Locher notes, such separation made it impossible for Zwingli to provide the theological foundation for the preaching which he gave so much prominence to.[125] At root, the problem was the same as the one that dogged his more general doctrine of God's sovereignty—he insisted upon the direct and unmediated causality of God.[126]

Bullinger

Bullinger was Zwingli's successor in Zurich, becoming the pastor of the city in 1531. While his writing lacked the flair of Zwingli's, it was noteworthy for its rigour and careful expression. His ministry was marked by stability and peaceful development compared with the more stormy times that dominated Zwingli's tenure and one of his key tasks, as he perceived it, was to strengthen the ties that existed between Zurich and other like-minded churches.[127] One of the ways he did this was through his participation in the formulation of the *First Helvetic Confession,* the *Second Helvetic Confession,* and the *Consensus Tigurinus.*

123 Locher, *Zwingli's Thought,* 15.
124 Stephens, *Theology of Zwingli,* 137.
125 Locher, *Zwingli's Thought,* 286.
126 Bromiley, *Zwingli and Bullinger,* 38.
127 Ibid., 43–44.

While Strivens (and indeed Luther) group Zwingli and Bullinger together, it is right to consider them separately because Bullinger diverged from Zwingli in several important ways. Firstly, in his understanding of the sacraments, Bullinger rejected pure memorialism (Zwingli's early view)[128] in favour of a form of symbolic parallelism (God works the reality alongside the sign), eventually incorporating this understanding into the wording of the *Second Helvetic Confession*.[129] Chapter XIX of the confession states that, in the sacraments, God 'offers unto our sight those things which inwardly he performs unto us, and therewithal strengthens and increases our faith through the working of God's Spirit in our hearts.'[130] In Chapter XXI, the confession declares of the Supper that 'he that outwardly does receive the sacrament with a true faith, the same does not only receive the sign, but also does enjoy the thing itself.'[131] Secondly, and relatedly, Bullinger insisted that the preached Word was the very Word of God and that its importance and fruitfulness was not undermined in any way by the necessity of the Spirit's inward illumination. Chapter I of the Confession states:

> Wherefore when this Word of God is now preached in the church by preachers lawfully called, we believe that the very Word of God is preached, and received of the faithful; and that neither any Word of God is to be feigned, nor to be expected from heaven: and that now the Word itself which is preached is to be regarded, not the minister that preaches; who, although he be evil and a sinner, nevertheless the Word of God abides true and good. Neither do we think that therefore the

128   There is evidence that Zwingli's view changed, see: B. A. Gerrish, *Grace and Gratitude: The Eucharistic Theology of John Calvin* (Minneapolis, MN: Fortress Press, 1993), 112, n. 111.

129   See ibid., 167; John Adger, 'Calvin Defended against Drs Cunningham and Hodge,' *The Southern Presbyterian Review* 27 (1876): 163; Ralph Cunnington, 'Calvin's Doctrine of the Lord's Supper,' *Westminster Theological Journal* 73 (2011): 220.

130   Schaff, *Creeds of Christendom*, 3:884

131   Ibid., 3:894.

outward preaching is to be thought as fruitless because the instruction in true religion depends on the inward illumination of the Spirit.[132]

Bullinger explicitly excluded the possibility of additional revelation (contra the radical Reformers) and while he recognised that the Spirit can illuminate whenever and whoever he wishes (as Luther himself recognised), even without the external ministry, he insisted that in preaching 'we speak of the usual way of instructing men, delivered unto us from God, both by commandment and examples.' This concession may indeed express a residual Zwinglian sentiment but, as Locher notes, Bullinger did not believe that one should begin with such exceptions: '[Bullinger] is less amazed at the power of the Spirit than at the miracle of the Word.'[133]

SUMMARY

In this chapter we have sought to evaluate the views of the early Reformers and have seen that they were far more complex than is often portrayed. While the revolutionary spiritualists certainly had a tendency to allow the Spirit to define the Word rather than the Word to define the Spirit,[134] there was variation among the main protagonists as to the extent to which they would appeal to fresh outpourings of revelation. Luther's position was also more complex than is sometimes suggested. While emphasising the unity of Word and Spirit and the importance of external means, he did not conflate them or teach that the power of the Spirit had been delegated to the Word. A tension ran throughout his work but it is impossible to resolve this tension simply by supposing a development which flowered into later Lutheranism. In truth, the tension continued throughout.

132   Ibid, 3:832.
133   Locher, *Zwingli's Thought*, 285.
134   Williams, *Spiritual and Anabaptist Writers*, 32.

In contrast to Luther, the early Swiss Reformers emphasised the need to distinguish Word and Spirit in an attempt to defend the sovereign freedom of God and the progress made by the Reformers in their battle against human traditions. This emphasis bordered upon separation at times in Zwingli and was directly linked to his understanding of the sacraments. Indeed, as we noted in our discussion of Luther, the sacramental quality of the Word meant that the Reformers' understanding of the relationship between Word and Spirit was often directly linked to their understanding of the sacraments. In light of this, in the next chapter we will begin our discussion of Calvin with a brief evaluation of his sacramental theology.

3

THE SPIRITUAL PRESENCE AND THE SUPPER

Just as Word and sacrament were closely connected in the theology of Luther and Zwingli, so too were they in Calvin's. Book IV of the *Institutes* is devoted to the church and the external means of grace. For Calvin, the fundamental means of grace are the preaching of the Word and the observance of the sacraments. Indeed, these are the distinguishing marks of a true church: 'Wherever we see the Word of God purely preached and heard, and the sacraments administered according to Christ's institution, there, it is not to be doubted, a church of God exists.'[1] Calvin goes further, insisting that the very presence of the marks ensures fruit since the marks 'can never exist without bringing forth fruit and prosperity by God's blessing.'[2] Calvin quickly qualified this statement by making clear that he does not

---

1   John Calvin, *Calvin: Institutes of the Christian Religion*, ed. McNeill, John T., trans. Battles, Ford Lewis, The Library of Christian Classics (Philadelphia, PA: The Westminster Press, 1960), 4.1.9.

2   Ibid., 4.1.10.

mean that the fruit will always be immediate but simply that the means of grace will always be shown to be effective.

For Calvin, Word and sacrament are inextricably linked. The efficacy of the sacraments depends entirely upon the sacramental word which accompanies them.[3] Indeed, according to Calvin, it is the Word that is indispensable to the sacramental action not the sign,[4] since 'God gives no more by visible signs than by His Word.'[5] While this might appear to imply that the sacraments are somehow of secondary importance, it is clear on further reading that Calvin assigned a very high place to the sacraments in the life of the church.[6] This was because of their capacity to present to the believer the promises of God's Word in 'a different manner' sensitive to our creaturely weakness.[7] As visible signs, they appeal to our limited capacities,[8] propping up our faith,[9] by presenting God's promises 'as painted in a picture from life.'[10]

Thus, while they differ in mode of operation, both the preaching of the Word and the administration of the sacraments

---

3   Calvin writes that the sacraments 'take their virtue from the Word, when it is preached intelligibly' (John Calvin, 'Short Treatise on the Holy Supper of Our Lord and Only Saviour Jesus Christ,' in *Calvin: Theological Treatises*, ed. J. K. S. Reid, Library of Christian Classics [Philadelphia, PA: Westminster Press, 1954], 161).

4   Gerrish, *Grace and Gratitude*, 162.

5   John Calvin, 'The Clear Explanation of Sound Doctrine Concerning the True Partaking of the Flesh and Blood of Christ in the Holy Supper,' in *Calvin: Theological Treatises*, ed. J. K. S. Reid, Library of Christian Classics (Philadelphia, PA: Westminster Press, 1954), 281.

6   Although assurance of salvation does not depend upon participation in them (Calvin, *Institutes*, 4.14.14; Calvin, 'Clear Explanation,' 291).

7   Calvin, 'Clear Explanation,' 281.

8   Calvin, *Institutes*, 4.17.1. See also John Calvin, *The Epistles of the Paul the Apostle to the Galatians, Ephesians, Philippians and Colossians*, ed. David W. Torrance and Thomas F. Torrance, trans. T.H.L. Parker, Calvin's New Testament Commentaries 11 (Grand Rapids, MI: Eerdmans, 1965), 206.

9   Calvin, *Institutes*, 4.14.3.

10   Ibid., 4.14.5.

fulfil the same office: they 'offer and set forth Christ to us, and in him the treasures of heavenly grace.'[11] Given this common office, there is good reason to believe that Calvin's understanding of the efficacy of the sacraments had a close bearing upon his understanding of the relationship between the Word and Spirit in preaching. In this chapter we will seek to trace out Calvin's understanding of the Sacraments with a view to establishing the foundations for our examination of Word and Spirit in preaching in the next.

WHAT IS A SACRAMENT?

Calvin defined a sacrament as 'an outward sign by which the Lord seals on our consciences the promises of his good will toward us in order to sustain the weakness of our faith; and we in turn attest our piety toward him in the presence of the Lord and of his angels and before men.'[12] This definition with its emphasis upon a sign and a seal that the Lord bestows upon the believer is in marked contrast to the position of Zwingli. In his 1525 work *von dem touff* ('On Baptism'), Zwingli wrote:

> As used in this context the word sacrament means a covenant sign or pledge. If a man sows on a white cross, he proclaims that he is a Confederate. And if he makes the pilgrimage to Nähenfels and gives God praise and thanksgiving for the victory vouchsafed to our father, he testifies that he is a Confederate indeed. Similarly the man who receives the mark of baptism is the one who is resolved to hear what God says to him, to learn the divine precepts and to live his life in accordance with them. And the man who in the remembrance of the Supper gives thanks to God in the congregation testifies to the fact that from the very heart he rejoices in the death of Christ and thanks him for it.[13]

11 Ibid., 4.14.17. See also: Calvin, 'Short Treatise,' 144.
12 Calvin, *Institutes*, 4.14.1.
13 Zwingli, 'On Baptism' in Bromiley, *Zwingli and Bullinger*, 131.

The background to Zwingli's analogy is the Swiss victory over the Austrians in 1388. The battle took place close to Nähenfels and marked the birth of the Swiss Confederacy. It was commemorated by an annual pilgrimage to the site of the battle.[14] Zwingli's analogy was twofold. Firstly, just as the Swiss Confederates wore a white cross to mark their allegiance to the Confederacy, so too do Christians pledge their allegiance to the church through baptism and the Lord's Supper: 'Baptism is a sign which pledges us to the Lord Jesus Christ.'[15] Secondly, just as the Swiss Confederates commemorate the event that brought the Confederacy into existence in their annual pilgrimage, so too do Christians commemorate the event that brought the church into existence (the death of the Lord Jesus) in their celebration of the Lord's Supper.

It is evident that, for Zwingli, the sacraments move from man towards God. They are signs by which believers pledge their allegiance towards God and the church. For Calvin, the movement is primarily in the opposite direction: from God towards believers. The sacraments constitute an 'outward attestation of the divine benevolence towards us, which represents spiritual grace symbolically, to seal the promises of God in our hearts, by which the truth of them is better confirmed.'[16] Thus, in baptism we have a testimony that we have been 'received into the family of God' and in the Supper 'God himself manifests himself to us as Father by feeding our souls.'[17] Calvin did not reject any movement the other way. Indeed, he explicitly agreed with Zwingli's view that the sacraments function as 'marks and as it were badges

---

14   Alister E. McGrath, ed., *The Christian Theology Reader*, 3rd ed. (Oxford: Blackwell Publishing, 2007), 577.

15   Bromiley, *Zwingli and Bullinger*, 131.

16   John Calvin, 'The Catechism of the Church in Geneva,' in *Calvin: Theological Treatises*, ed. J. K. S. Reid, Library of Christian Classics (Philadelphia, PA: Westminster Press, 1954), 131.

17   Ibid., 133.

of our profession.'[18] They are both a 'testimony of divine grace toward us' and a 'mutual attestation of our piety toward him.'[19] The difference is that, for Calvin, Zwingli's view is a secondary and subordinate purpose of the sacraments.[20] As Gerrish notes, for Calvin, 'Zwingli has the priorities wrong. Indeed, he not only put first what can only be secondary but made it the whole sacrament; he imagined that a sacrament is only an act by which we attest out faith and not rather, as it truly is, a sign by which God strengthens our faith.'[21]

SIGN AND REALITY

Zwingli maintained that his opponents (he primarily had Luther and Rome in view) had fallen into error by conflating the sign (either through consubstantiation[22] (Luther) or transubstantiation[23] (Rome)) with the thing signified: 'if they are the things which they signify they are no longer signs; for sign and thing signified cannot be the same thing.'[24] For Calvin, Zwingli had himself fallen into error by illegitimately separating the sign from the thing signified. This had dangerous implications because it rendered the sign 'bare' and called into question God's truthfulness. Calvin writes: '[T]he sacraments of the Lord ought not and cannot at all be separated from their reality and substance. To distinguish them so that they be not confused is not only good

18   Ibid., 138. See also Calvin, *Institutes*, 4.14.13.

19   Calvin, *Institutes*, 4.14.1.

20   Calvin writes: 'we do not tolerate that what is secondary in the sacraments be regarded by them as the first and even the only point' (Ibid., 4.14.13).

21   Gerrish, *Grace and Gratitude*, 8.

22   The view that Christ's body is physically present 'in, with and under' the elements.

23   The view that the elements are transformed into the physical body and blood of Christ.

24   Bromiley, *Zwingli and Bullinger*, 131.

and reasonable but wholly necessary. But to divide them so as to set them up the one without the other is absurd…If God cannot deceive or lie, it follows that he performs all that it signifies.'[25]

Calvin expanded upon this in his commentary on I Corinthians 10:3, where he observed that the provision of manna in the desert corresponded to the Lord's Supper since the 'fathers ate the same spiritual meat.' These sacraments, like their New Covenant equivalents were not 'bare forms' since 'the reality figured is truly given at the same time. For God is not so deceitful as to nourish us on empty appearances.'[26] Calvin used the Christological maxim 'distinct but not separate' to explain the relationship between sign and reality and to indicate where others had fallen into error.[27] Rome 'confound the reality and the sign', failing to properly observe the distinction that exists, while 'unbelievers such as Schwenkfeld and men like him separate the signs from the realities.' Calvin preferred a 'middle position' thus preserving 'the union made by the Lord,' while also maintaining a clear 'distinction between' the sign and its corresponding reality.[28] Although Calvin did not directly refer to Zwingli, it is clear that his criticism applies with equal force to Zwingli's view.

25   Calvin, 'Short Treatise,' 147–148. See also: John Calvin, *The First Epistle of Paul the Apostle to the Corinthians*, ed. David W. Torrance and Thomas F. Torrance, trans. Johnston, William B., Calvin's New Testament Commentaries (Grand Rapids, MI: Eerdmans, 1996), 245.

26   Calvin, *I Corinthians*, 203.

27   The maxim is found in the Chalcedonian Definition: '… one and the same Christ, Son, Lord, Only-begotten, recognized in two natures, without confusion, without change, without division, without *separation*; the *distinction* of natures being in no way annulled by the union, but rather the characteristics of each nature being preserved and coming together to form one person and subsistence, not as parted or *separated* into two persons, but one and the same Son and Only-begotten God the Word…' (emphasis added).

28   Calvin, *I Corinthians*, 203. See also Calvin, *Institutes*, 4.14.15.

WAYS AND MEANS

The stumbling point for Zwingli and the reason why he could not accept that the sacraments were a means of grace was his concern that such a position would bind the Spirit to the use of outward means. As we have seen, this is the very concern that caused Zwingli to separate Word and Spirit at times. In *An Account of the Faith*, Zwingli insisted that the sacraments do not confer grace because it is for the Spirit alone to confer grace: '[A] channel or vehicle is not necessary to the Spirit, for he himself is the virtue and energy whereby all things are borne, and has no need of being borne.'[29] In a similar vein, he maintained that the sacraments do not and cannot confirm faith because 'it is not possible for an external thing to confirm faith. For faith does not proceed from external things.'[30] Zwingli was concerned to emphasise that the Spirit neither needs nor is bound to outward means.[31] He can work in whatever way he chooses and cannot be contained or controlled.

Calvin had no such concerns, insisting that 'God uses means and instruments which he himself sees to be expedient, that all things may serve his glory, since he is Lord and Judge of all.'[32] He was also happy to speak about the sacraments as confirming our faith, noting that when God wishes to take away our confidence in the promises signified by the sacraments, he removes the sacraments themselves. The withdrawal of the tree of life following Adam's loss of immortality at the Fall is cited as an example.[33]

Calvin is aware that God's use of external means in the sacraments may be taken to detract from his glory but to counter

29   Cited in: Stephens, *Theology of Zwingli*, 186.
30   Bromiley, *Zwingli and Bullinger*, 138.
31   See discussion in: Robert Letham, 'Baptism in the Writings of the Reformers,' *The Scottish Bulletin of Evangelical Theology* 7.1 (1989): 24–25.
32   Calvin, *Institutes*, 4.14.12.
33   Ibid.

this he points to God's use of external means elsewhere. Just as God feeds us physically through bread and other foods, so he feeds us spiritually through the sacraments. We do not put confidence in the food that he provides nor admire it or proclaim it to be the cause of our good. Likewise, we ought not to let our confidence rest 'in the sacraments, nor the glory of God be transferred to them.'[34] Calvin insists that, 'whatever instruments [God] uses, these detract nothing from his original activity.'[35]

Far from detracting from God's glory, Calvin was convinced that God's use of external means in the sacraments was a crucial accommodation to our creaturely weakness that enabled us to appreciate the goodness of his promises in Christ. In the Geneva Catechism, the minister asks the catechumen why God uses such external means in the sacraments. He replies:

> By this means he has consideration on our weakness. For if we were wholly spiritual like the angels, we should be able to see both him and his gifts. But as we are surrounded by this gross earthly body, we need symbols or mirrors, to exhibit to us the appearance of spiritual and heavenly things in a kind of earthly way. For we could not otherwise attain to them. At the same time it is to our interest that all our senses be exercised in the promises of God, by which they are better confirmed to us.[36]

THE RELATIONSHIP BETWEEN SIGN AND REALITY

Gerrish has suggested that, within the Reformed tradition, there are three different conceptions of the relationship between sacramental signs and the reality to which they point: symbolic memorialism, symbolic parallelism and symbolic instrumentalism.[37]

---

34   Ibid.
35   Ibid., 4.14.17.
36   Calvin, 'Geneva Catechism,' 131.
37   Gerrish, *Grace and Gratitude*, 167.

The component shared by all three conceptions is that the sacrament is a sign that points to something else.

Symbolic memorialism is typified by Zwingli's view in which the sacrament points to something that has happened in the past. For Zwingli, the Lord's Supper was simply a memorial of the cross: 'the bread is only a figure of his body to remind us in the Supper that the body was crucified for us.'[38] Symbolic parallelism views the reality as happening simultaneously in the present.[39] In symbolic instrumentalism, the emphasis is upon the reality actually being brought about through the sign.[40]

The three conceptions are by no means mutually exclusive and all three are present in Calvin's work. In places, he adopts memorialist language, speaking of the Supper as 'a mirror in which we contemplate our Lord Jesus Christ crucified to abolish our faults and offences.'[41] In others, he emphasises parallelism: 'as bread nourishes, sustains, and keeps the life of our body, so Christ's body is the only food to invigorate and enliven our soul.'[42] The language of parallelism is also present in his discussion of baptism: God washes away our sins and wipes out the remembrance of them just as 'surely as we see our body outwardly cleansed, submerged and surrounded with water.'[43] But as Gerrish notes,

38   Zwingli, 'On the Lord's Supper' in Bromiley, *Zwingli and Bullinger*, 225. It seems that Zwingli may have moved away from a purely memorialist view later in his life. In 'An Exposition of the Faith,' Zwingli wrote 'To eat the body of Christ sacramentally is to eat the body of Christ with the heart and the mind in conjunction with the sacrament' (Ibid., 258).

39   It was the position adopted by Heinrich Bullinger and Robert Bruce. See: Gerrish, *Grace and Gratitude*, 166–168; Robert Bruce, *The Mystery of the Lord's Supper: Sermons on the Sacrament Preached in the Kirk of Edinburgh*, ed. Thomas F. Torrance, 2nd ed. (Edinburgh: Rutherford House, 2005), 77–81, 90–92.

40   Gerrish, *Grace and Gratitude*, 167.

41   Calvin, 'Short Treatise,' 145. See also Calvin, *Institutes*, 4.17.37.

42   Calvin, *Institutes*, 4.17.3. See also ibid., 4.17.5. See discussion in: Gerrish, *Grace and Gratitude*, 166–167, n. 29.

43   Calvin, *Institutes*, 4.15.14.

an understanding of Calvin's sacramental theology is incomplete without recognising the importance of instrumentalism.[44] According to Calvin, the bread and wine of the Supper are called the body and blood 'because they are as *instruments* by which our Lord Jesus Christ distributes them to us.'[45] In the *Institutes*, he teaches that though the elements are symbolic we can 'duly infer that by the showing of the symbol the thing itself is shown.'[46]

EX OPERE OPERATO?

All this necessarily raises the question of whether Calvin's instrumentalism collapsed into a repackaged doctrine of *ex opere operato*? The answer of course is no, since Calvin was insistent that the grace of the sacrament resides, not in the sacrament itself, but in the cross of Christ to which it points.[47] It is Christ himself who is the true food for our soul, and the sacrament simply reminds us 'that he was made the bread of life, which we continually eat and which gives us relish and savor of that bread, it causes us to feel the power of that bread.'[48]

To rightly understand the efficacy of the sacraments in Calvin's thinking, we must grasp that the efficacy and power emanates from the Holy Spirit who joins his virtue to the sacraments 'when they are duly received.'[49] They are not efficacious for all but only for those who come with faith and repentance.[50] Separation of faith from the sacraments is, according to Calvin, tantamount to

---

44   Gerrish, *Grace and Gratitude*, 167.

45   Calvin, 'Short Treatise,' 147 (my emphasis).

46   Calvin, *Institutes*, 4.17.10.

47   Calvin, 'Short Treatise,' 157.

48   Calvin, *Institutes*, 4.17.1,5.

49   Calvin, 'Short Treatise,' 149. See also Calvin, *Galatians, Ephesians, Philippians and Colossians*, 203.

50   Calvin, 'Short Treatise,' 150.

taking the soul away from the body, [51] for a person takes away from the sacrament 'no more than they gather with the vessel of faith.'[52]

ARE THE SACRAMENTS
EVER UNACCOMPANIED BY THE SPIRIT?

We come to a number of questions which will significantly impact our understanding of the relationship between Word and Spirit. Within Calvin's theology, are the sacraments ever separated from the reality to which they point? Are they ever unaccompanied by the Spirit? Do they cease to function as a means of grace simply by virtue of their not being received with faith?

We will begin with the latter question since it is the most straightforward and is addressed directly by Calvin in the *Institutes*. There, he notes that the reasoning which lies behind such a question is flawed because the same argument could be used to assert that Christ and the gospel are not testimonies of God's grace since the gospel is heard but rejected by many and Christ was seen but accepted by few.[53]

We must next consider whether the sacraments are ever unaccompanied by the Holy Spirit. This is linked to the prior question of whether the reality is ever separated from the sign and is a difficult question to answer. On the one hand, Calvin is clear that the sacraments are not efficacious without the work of the Holy Spirit. He writes: 'the sacraments properly fulfil their office only when the Spirit, that inward teacher, comes to them, by whose power alone hearts are penetrated and affections moved and our souls opened for the sacraments to enter in.'[54]

---

51 'Antidote to the Council of Trent' in John Calvin, *John Calvin: Selections from His Writings*, ed. John Dillenberger (Garden City, NY: Anchor Books, 1971), 213.

52 Calvin, *Institutes*, 4.17.33.

53 Ibid., 4.14.7.

54 Ibid., 4.14.9.

Calvin compares receipt of the sacraments to seeing the sun or hearing a voice. If the Spirit is lacking it is like seeing with blind eyes or hearing with deaf ears. Calvin writes: 'what sight does in our eyes for seeing light, and what hearing does in our ears for perceiving a voice, are analogous to the work of the Holy Spirit in our hearts, which is to conceive, sustain, nourish, and establish faith.'[55] The power rests with the Spirit while the ministry is left to the sacraments. Moreover, the Holy Spirit is not given indiscriminately to all men.[56]

On the face of it, this sounds like Calvin is suggesting that the sacraments and the Spirit can be separated. He even speaks about making a division between Spirit and sacraments.[57] But caution is needed here. We have already seen that Calvin employed the Christological maxim 'distinct but not separate' to explain the relationship between sign and reality in the sacraments. He insisted that the reality of the sacrament is *always* present and available with the sign for those who come with faith.[58] Moreover, he was alert to correct the view that the sacraments are nullified by the unfaithfulness of the recipients. Calvin insisted that 'what God has ordained remains firm and keeps its own nature, however men may vary.'[59] In other words, the sacrament remains what it is; it simply does not benefit unbelievers. Calvin quoted Augustine with approval: 'If you receive carnally, it does not cease to be spiritual, but it is not so for you.'[60]

In respect of baptism, Calvin maintained that the Lord does not present us with a mere appearance only; rather he

---

55   Ibid. See also: Ibid., 4.14.17.

56   Calvin, *Institutes*, 4.14.17.

57   Ibid., 4.14.9.

58   Calvin, 'Short Treatise,' 147–148, 163; Calvin, *1 Corinthians*, 203.

59   Calvin, *Institutes*, 4.14.16.

60   Augustine, John Saint Augustine, 'Tractates on John,' in *Nicene and Post-Nicene Fathers Series 1–07*, ed. Philip Schaff (London: T & T Clark, 1980), 176. Cited in: Calvin, *Institutes*, 4.14.16.

'leads us to the present reality and effectively performs what it symbolises.'[61] Likewise, in respect of the Supper he is clear that the unfaithfulness of communicants takes nothing away from the sacrament: 'its truth and effectiveness remain undiminished, although the wicked go away empty after outward participation in it.'[62] Elsewhere, '[i]f God cannot deceive or lie, it follows that he performs all that it signifies.'[63] The sacrament retains its nature and continues to present the body and blood of Christ whether it is received with faith or not. It is like rain falling on a hard rock which flows off because there is no entrance for it.

To summarise, Calvin affirms three truths. Firstly, the sacraments are not efficacious without the work of the Spirit. Secondly, the sacraments retain their essential nature as a means of grace regardless of whether they are of benefit to those who receive them. The reality remains inseparable from the sign even if the reality is not received with the sign. Thirdly, the reality is *always* available with the sign if it is received with Spirit-wrought faith.

It is this final statement which is crucial. While it is clear that Calvin distinguished the Spirit from the sacraments in such a way so as to affirm that it is possible to receive the sacraments without receiving the Spirit, he did not in any way suggest that the Spirit's accompaniment of the sacraments was only sporadic or unpredictable. His point was simply that, since the sacraments may be received by those who have not themselves received the Spirit, it is possible for the sacraments to be received only sacramentally and not in reality.[64] In other words, the Spirit may accompany the sacraments in judgment rather than blessing.[65]

---

61   Calvin, *Institutes*, 4.15.14.

62   Ibid., 4.17.33.

63   Calvin, 'Short Treatise,' 148.

64   Calvin, *Institutes*, 4.17.34. Calvin writes: 'Now if a man has not a vestige of living faith or of repentance, and nothing of the Spirit of Christ, how can he receive Christ himself?' (*1 Corinthians*, 251).

65   Calvin, *Institutes*, 4.17.40.

Contrary to Rome, Calvin insisted that the sacraments do not bring the Spirit indiscriminately to all men. Rather, it is the Lord who bestows the Holy Spirit on his people,[66] and those who have received the Spirit can approach the sacraments with confidence knowing that, through their Spirit-wrought faith, they may receive the reality with the sacrament. As Calvin writes in his commentary on Romans 6:4, we must always speak of the reality subsisting with the sacrament 'while the institution of the Lord and the faith of the believers correspond, for we never have naked and empty symbols, except when our ingratitude and wickedness hinder the working of the divine beneficence.'[67]

In conclusion, although the sacraments may be received apart from the Spirit (thus only sacramentally) this is due to the unbelief of the recipient; not to any unwillingness of the Spirit to accompany the sacraments in blessing or to any deception in the sacraments themselves. In the sacraments Christ 'is certainly offered in common to all, unbelievers as well as believers.'[68] The reality to which the sacraments point is always available with the sign to any who come with faith and the power of the sacraments is in no way diminished by their being received by unbelievers.

---

66   Ibid., 4.14.17.

67   John Calvin, *The Epistles of Paul the Apostle to the Romans and to the Thessalonians*, ed. David W. Torrance and Thomas F. Torrance, trans. Ross Mackenzie, Calvin's New Testament Commentaries (Grand Rapids, MI: Eerdmans, 1973), 123.

68   Calvin, 'Clear Explanation,' 316.

4

THE SPIRIT-ACCOMPANIED WORD

In the previous chapter we saw how Calvin employed the Christological maxim, 'distinct but not separate' to describe the relationship between the sacramental signs and the reality to which they point. While the sacraments are never efficacious apart from the work of the Holy Spirit, they do not lose their essential nature by virtue of their not being received with faith. This means that the grace to which they point is always available with the sign when received with Spirit-wrought faith. In this chapter we turn to consider the relationship between Word and Spirit in preaching and it quickly becomes apparent that the relationships are analogous. The same questions arise. Is the Word ever separated from the power of the Gospel? Is the preaching of the Word ever unaccompanied by the Spirit? Does the Word cease to function as a means of grace simply by virtue of it not being received with faith?

As we saw in chapter one, Robert Strivens suggests that Calvin separated Word and Spirit so that the two are not tied together irrevocably.[1] In Strivens' reading of Calvin, while the preacher may rightly expect the Spirit to be at work when the Word is preached, 'the Spirit does not necessarily and in every case give efficacy to the Word' and sometimes 'the Word can be preached in a manner that is bereft of the Spirit.'[2] In this chapter, we will scrutinise those statements to ascertain whether they accurately reflect the full tenor of Calvin's thought as expressed in the Institutes, his commentaries and other writings.

GOD'S WORD AND THE PREACHED WORD

At the outset, it is important to grasp the relationship between God's Word and the preached Word in Calvin's thinking.[3] Calvin understood that God ordinarily uses means to communicate with his people.[4] This has been God's pattern throughout his dealings with humanity, 'for God does not speak openly from heaven, but employs men as his instruments, that by their agency he may make known his will.'[5] Under the Old Covenant, God used prophets for this purpose and enabled them to speak his words with his own power and authority. Commenting on Haggai 1:12, Calvin wrote:

> [T]he people received not what they heard from the mouth of mortal man, otherwise than if the majesty of God had openly appeared. For there was no ocular view of God given; but the message of the Prophet obtained as much power as though God had descended

1 Strivens, 'Preaching,' 65.

2 Ibid., 64–65.

3 See further Ronald S. Wallace, *Calvin's Doctrine of the Word and Sacrament* (Edinburgh: Scottish Academic Press, 1995), 82–84.

4 Calvin writes: 'For although God's power is not bound to outward means, he has nonetheless bound us to the ordinary manner of teaching' (Calvin, *Institutes*, 4.1.5).

5 John Calvin, *Commentary on the Book of the Prophet Isaiah: Volume 4*, trans. William Pringle (Edinburgh: Calvin Translation Society, 1854), 172.

from heaven, and had given manifest tokens of his presence. We may then conclude from these words, that the glory of God so shines in his word, that we ought to be so much affected by it, whenever he speaks by his servants, as though he were nigh to us, face to face, as the Scripture says in another place.[6]

Today, God speaks through ministers who have been commissioned to faithfully expound the Scripture.[7] Such ministers speak on the same basis as the prophets of Israel since, 'if they derogate nothing from the authority of God, it follows that none except the only true God ought to be heard.'[8] Indeed, 'where preaching is, there God's voice ringeth in our ears.'[9] Ministers of the Word are the fundamental channel through which God's Word is communicated to his people. God 'does not wish to be heard but by the voice of his minister'[10] and he 'does not speak Himself, but through men.'[11] So close is the relationship between Christ and his ministers that in the parable of the sower 'Christ claims for Himself what in a sense He shares with His ministers.'[12] It can be said that Christ sows the seed of his Word when his ministers preach because they are 'like His hand.' When the gospel is preached we should not think of it being told by the men themselves but 'by

6   John Calvin, *Commentaries on the Twelve Minor Prophets, Volume 4: Habakkuk, Zephaniah, Haggai*, trans. John Owen (Edinburgh: Calvin Translation Society, 1848), 342–343.

7   Calvin, *Institutes*, 4.1.5.

8   Hag 1:12

9   John Calvin, *Sermons on Deuteronomy*, trans. Arthur Golding (Edinburgh: Banner of Truth Trust, 1987), 1206.

10   Calvin, *Isaiah Vol. 4*, 61.

11   John Calvin, *The Epistle of Paul the Apostle to the Hebrews and the First and Second Epistles of St Peter*, ed. David W. Torrance and Thomas F. Torrance, trans. William B. Johnston (Edinburgh: Oliver & Boyd, 1963), 52.

12   John Calvin, *A Harmony of the Gospels, Matthew, Mark and Luke: Volume 2*, ed. David W. Torrance and Thomas F. Torrance, trans. T.H.L. Parker (Grand Rapids, MI: Eerdmans, 1972), 76.

Christ with their lips.'[13] Elsewhere Calvin speaks of the ministry of the Word as a 'sort of delegated work' whereby he uses the preachers' mouths to do his own work, much like a workman uses a tool.[14] When the ministers faithfully declare the words of Christ, their mouth is his mouth and their lips are his lips.[15]

It is clear that just as God is present whenever the sacraments are administered, so too God is present whenever the Word is preached. In the *Institutes*, Calvin teaches that the sacraments and the Word have the same office: 'to offer and set forth Christ to us and in him the treasures of heavenly grace.'[16] The connection is highlighted in Calvin's *Short Treatise on the Supper*. It is in Christ that the fullness of life is communicated but the instrument that God has ordained to dispense Christ and his benefits to us is the Word.[17] It is through his Word that God reveals himself to those he wishes to call,[18] and through the preaching of the Word that God 'stretches forth his hands to us exactly as a father stretches forth his arms, ready to receive his son lovingly into his bosom.'[19] When the Word is preached God approaches his people and gives to them the very token of his presence.[20] Commenting on Cornelius' experience of receiving the Word from Peter in Acts 10:33, Calvin writes that, whenever the Word is set before

13   Calvin, *Hebrews, 1 & 2 Peter*, 27.

14   Calvin, *Institutes*, 4.3.1. See also H. Jackson Forstman, *Word and Spirit. Calvin's Doctrine of Biblical Authority* (Stanford, CA: Stanford University Press, 1962), 78.

15   John Calvin, *Commentary on the Book of the Prophet Isaiah: Volume 1*, trans. William Pringle (Edinburgh: Calvin Translation Society, 1850), 381.

16   Calvin, *Institutes*, 4.14.17.

17   Calvin, 'Short Treatise,' 143. Calvin immediately notes the connection to the sacraments observing that 'what is said of the Word fitly belongs also to the sacrament of the Supper, by means of which our Lord leads us to communion with Jesus Christ' (Ibid., 144). See also Calvin, *Hebrews, 1 & 2 Peter*, 254.

18   Calvin, *Institutes*, 4.3.2.

19   Calvin, *Romans and Thessalonians*, 236–237.

20   Calvin, *Isaiah Vol. 4*, 50.

us, we ought to recognise that 'God is present and calling us.'[21] Describing Calvin's understanding of preaching as a sign of the presence of God, Ronald Wallace writes: 'Through the preaching of the Word by His ministers, Christ therefore gives His sacramental presence in the midst of His Church, imparts to men the grace which the Word promises, and establishes His Kingdom over the hearts of His hearers.'[22]

THE POWER OF THE WORD

Given the close relationship between God's Word and the preached Word it is important to ascertain exactly what Calvin understood the power and efficacy of the Word to be. Calvin was convinced that the Word is always effective to achieve its purpose. Commenting on Isaiah 55:10, he wrote: 'if we see great efficacy in the rain, which waters and fertilises the earth, much greater efficacy will God display in his word.'[23] Calvin was careful though to elaborate upon what such efficacy looks like. He recognised that some understood the text to mean that the preaching of the gospel always yields some fruit. He affirmed the truth of this statement but opined that it was not Isaiah's primary meaning.[24] Rather, the prophet's focus was on the fact that God's words are never spoken in vain; his promises are never merely scattered into the air. We will actually 'receive the fruit of them, provided that we do not prevent it by our unbelief.'[25] This

21   John Calvin, *The Acts of the Apostles Volume 1*, ed. David W. Torrance and Thomas F. Torrance, trans. W. J. G. McDonald (Grand Rapids, MI: Eerdmans, 1979), 305.

22   Wallace, *Word and Sacrament*, 84.

23   Calvin, *Isaiah Vol. 4*, 171.

24   Elsewhere, Calvin declares that Christ does not wish the labour of his ministers to be fruitless (*Isaiah Vol. 1*, 381).

25   Calvin, *Isaiah Vol. 4*, 171.

conditional aspect of efficacy is important and we shall return to it below.

A key passage on the efficacy of God's Word is Calvin's commentary on Hebrews 4:12. In it, he makes several important observations concerning the different effects of God's Word upon its listeners to which we shall return below. All we need to note at present is the general tenor of his comments. Calvin maintained that '[i]f anyone thinks that the air echoes with an empty sound when the Word of God is sent forth, he is making a great mistake. This was something alive, and full of hidden power which leaves nothing in man untouched.'[26] Once more, Calvin insists that God's Word is not scattered in vain; nor does he allow it to fall to the ground neglected. Instead he has 'imbued His Word with...power' so that it searches out every part of the soul and scrutinises our thoughts.[27] There is no obstruction too powerful to prevent the Word from doing its work; 'there is nothing so hard or firm in a man, nothing so deeply hidden that the efficacy of the Word, does not penetrate through to it.'[28]

For Calvin, the efficacy of the Word resides in the matter that the Word contains, namely the death and resurrection of Christ.[29] When James speaks of the Word being able to save (James 1:21), Calvin assures us that James does not mean that salvation is received merely through the outward hearing of the Word, as if God's saving task were being put into the hands of others. Rather James speaks of 'the Word which penetrates, by faith, to the heart of man, and means only that God, as Author of salvation, accomplishes this by the agency of His own Gospel.'[30]

---

26   Calvin, *Hebrews, 1 & 2 Peter*, 51.

27   Ibid.

28   Ibid., 53.

29   Calvin, *2 Corinthians, Timothy, Titus and Philemon*, 298.

30   John Calvin, *A Harmony of the Gospels, Matthew, Mark and Luke: Volume 3 and the Epistles of James and Jude*, ed. David W. Torrance and Thomas F. Torrance, trans. A. W. Morrison (Grand Rapids, MI: Eerdmans, 1972), 272.

In describing the efficacy of the Word, Calvin adopted language familiar to contemporary speech act theory.[31] God's Word is inseparable from His action. He does what he says and his words have both illocutionary and perlocutionary force. Calvin expresses this understanding of the effect of God's Word in his commentary on Romans 3:4: '*God*…is *true*, not only because He is prepared to stand faithfully by His promises, but also because He fulfils in deed whatever He declares in Word; for He says, "As my power, so also shall my work be".'[32] In commenting on the words of Isaiah, 'For the mouth of the Lord has commanded' (Isa. 34:16), Calvin writes, 'nothing that comes out of God's holy mouth can fail of its effect.'[33] Whatever God has decreed *will* come to pass and it cannot be reversed. The same point is made in Calvin's discussion of the rendering of *dunamis* (power) in 1 Thessalonnians 1:5. He recognises that some take *dunamis* to refer to miracles but he prefers the view that it refers to the spiritual power of doctrine. While the eloquence of man is often lifeless and empty, the living voice of God is 'inseparable from its effect.'[34] Commenting upon the words of Isaiah 34:16, 'For the mouth of the Lord has commanded', Calvin insists that nothing that comes forth out of God's mouth can 'fail of its effect.'[35] God's words are never 'thrown away and ineffectual.'[36] They do what they declare.

31   On speech act theory see: J. L. Austin, *How to Do Things with Words* (Oxford: Clarendon Press, 1962); John R. Searle, *Speech Acts: An Essay in the Philosophy of Language* (Cambridge: Cambridge University Press, 1970); Timothy Ward, *Word and Supplement: Speech Acts, Biblical Texts, and the Sufficiency of Scripture* (Oxford: Oxford University Press, 2002).

32   Calvin, *Romans and Thessalonians*, 60.

33   Calvin, *Isaiah Vol. 3*, 58.

34   Calvin, *Romans and Thessalonians*, 336.

35   Calvin, *Isaiah Vol. 3*, 58.

36   John Calvin, *Commentaries on the Four Last Books of Moses, Arranged in the Form of a Harmony Volume 4*, trans. Charles William Bingham (Edinburgh: Calvin Translation Society, 1855), 328.

This still leaves open the question of whether this performative efficacy of the Word is in effect whenever the Word is preached. In his discussion of Paul's comments on the work of ministers in 1 Corinthians 3, Calvin notes that Paul speaks of ministers in two ways. Sometimes he speaks of them so as to emphasise the efficacy of their work as ministers of the Spirit. But at other times, he emphasises, as in 1 Corinthians 3:7, that ministers are nothing but instruments of God, dependent on the Lord for effective power. Even here, however, Calvin is quick to remind his readers that 'Christ puts forth his own power in the ministry which He instituted, in such a way that it is evident that it was not instituted in vain...His power is made known as efficacious in the minister.'[37]

Calvin makes similar observations in his commentary on Malachi 4:6, noting that when God speaks highly of his ministers, the power of the Spirit is not excluded. Indeed, when he transfers to the minister that which is his own (efficacy), he does so in a way that it never ceases to dwell in him: 'he never resigns to them his own office, but makes them partakers of it only.'[38] Calvin is always careful to distinguish between Christ and the minister, emphasising that Christ does not take away anything from himself. This is important in understanding the relationship between efficacy and the preacher but we will defer our discussion of that to a later point.

THE SOURCE OF THE WORD'S POWER

In the previous chapter we saw that, in Calvin's understanding, the efficacy and power of the sacraments resides wholly in the Holy Spirit who joins his virtue to the sacraments whenever

37   Calvin, *1 Corinthians*. See also the discussion in Wallace, *Word and Sacrament*, 88.

38   John Calvin, *Commentaries on the Twelve Minor Prophets, Volume 5: Zechariah and Malachi*, trans. John Owen (Edinburgh: Calvin Translation Society, 1849), 629.

they are properly received.[39] Exactly the same can be said of the preaching of the Word. The efficacy of the Word is to be ascribed to the Holy Spirit.[40] 'Preaching would be of little use, if God did not give power and efficacy to his doctrine by the Spirit.'[41] In giving efficacy to the Word, the Spirit enables mortal voices to become instruments of eternal life.[42] Calvin writes: 'Certainly God works effectively through his Word, but we must affirm that its efficacy is not contained in the sound itself but comes from the hidden power of the Spirit.'[43] In his Isaiah commentary, Calvin writes: 'without the efficacy of the Spirit, the preaching of the gospel would avail nothing, but would remain unfruitful.'[44] This explains why, according to Calvin, the Prophet in Ezekiel 2:2 was not raised up until the Spirit stood him on his feet: 'the external Word is of no importance by itself, unless it is animated by the power of the Spirit.'[45] This obviously has important implications for our understanding of the relationship between the Word and Spirit to which we shall return.

Just as Calvin was convinced that Scripture was composed under the divine and infallible inspiration of the Holy Spirit, so he believed that it could only be rightly understood through the divine illumination of the Spirit.[46] 'Without the illumination

39   Calvin, 'Short Treatise,' 149. See also Calvin, *Galatians, Ephesians, Philippians and Colossians*, 203.

40   Calvin, *Hebrews, 1 & 2 Peter*, 52.

41   Calvin, *Isaiah Vol. 4*, 165.

42   Calvin, *Hebrews, 1 & 2 Peter*, 255.

43   John Calvin, *Ezekiel 1 (Chapters 1–12)*, trans. David Foxgrover and Donald Martin (Grand Rapids, MI: William B. Eerdmans, 1994), 59.

44   Calvin, *Isaiah Vol. 4*, 271.

45   Calvin, *Ezekiel 1–12*, 59.

46   See my discussion of Calvin's doctrine of inspiration in: Ralph Cunnington, 'Did Turretin Depart from Calvin's View on the Concept of Error in the Scriptures?,' *Foundations* 61 (2011): 41–58. See also: Gwyn Walters, *The Sovereign Spirit: The Doctrine of the Holy Spirit in the Writings of John Calvin*, ed. Eifion Evans and Lynn Quigley (Edinburgh: Rutherford House, 2009), 24–40.

of the Holy Spirit, the Word can do nothing.'[47] By nature, all of us are blind to the truth of Scripture. This is not due to the nature of the Word itself but is 'accidental' to the Word and is wholly attributable to the depravity of man.[48] As a consequence of this depravity, our eyes are 'veiled and shut' and in need of 'the invisible grace' of the Holy Spirit to open them.[49] Calvin described the Holy Spirit as the inner teacher 'by whose effort the promise of salvation penetrates into our minds, a promise that would otherwise only strike the air or bear upon our ears.'[50] In his commentary on Psalm 119, Calvin writes: 'It would profit us little to have the divine law sounding in our ears, or to have it exhibited in writing before our eyes, and to have it expounded by the voice of man, did not God correct our slowness of apprehension, and render us docile by the secret influence of his Spirit.'[51]

Similarly, when commenting upon Jesus's encounter with his disciples on the road to Emmaus, Calvin writes '[w]ords float into thin air to no effect, until minds are illuminated with the gift of understanding.' He compares the Word to a lantern, claiming that it merely shines in the darkness and among the blind 'until the inner light is shed upon their eyes by the Lord.'[52] Scriptural teaching is of no effect until 'the Spirit shapes our minds to understand it, and our hearts to accept it.'[53] In discussing the

---

47   Calvin, *Institutes*, 3.2.33.

48   Calvin, *Isaiah Vol. 1*, 217.

49   John Calvin, *Commentary on the Book of Psalms Volume 4*, trans. James Anderson (Edinburgh: Calvin Translation Society, 1847), 413.

50   Calvin, *Institutes*, 3.1.4.

51   John Calvin, *Commentary on the Book of Psalms Volume 5*, trans. James Anderson (Edinburgh: Calvin Translation Society, 1849), 5.

52   Calvin, *Harmony of the Gospels Vol. 3, James and Jude*, 245. Calvin insists that Christ inwardly addresses our hearts by His Spirit (*The Gospel According to John: Volume 2*, ed. David W. Torrance and Thomas F. Torrance, trans. T.H.L. Parker, Calvin's New Testament Commentaries [Grand Rapids, MI: Eerdmans, 1961], 131).

53   Calvin, *Harmony of the Gospels Vol. 3, James and Jude*, 245.

Spirit's role of convicting the world of sin, Calvin asks how it can be that the voice of a man can penetrate minds, take root and bear fruit and turn hearts of stone into hearts of flesh. The answer is 'because the Spirit of Christ quickens it.' Men have no power of their own; they are merely instruments over whom the Spirit presides.[54]

The importance of the efficacy of the Word residing in the Spirit is also evident in Calvin's commentary on 2 Corinthians 4:6. Calvin notes that Paul employs the language of creation to describe how God works when the Word is preached. Just as in creation God gave brightness to the sun and eyes to mankind to see it, 'so in our redemption He shines forth upon us in the person of His Son by His Gospel, but that would be in vain, since we are blind, unless He were also to illuminate our minds by His Spirit.'[55] Again, it is evident that the efficacy of the Word resides with the Spirit, just as Calvin explicitly observed a few pages earlier in the commentary.[56] But equally it is clear that, for Calvin, the Word and the Spirit are inextricably connected in the proclamation of the Gospel. The Word without the illuminating work of the Spirit would be like the sun shining onto blind eyes and the Spirit without the radiance of the Word would be like healthy eyes staring into a dark abyss. This brings us to the central question of the relationship that Calvin understood to exist between the Word and Spirit in preaching.

WORD AND SPIRIT

As we saw in our opening chapter, Robert Strivens has argued that, although Calvin believed in a very close relationship between Word and Spirit, he 'did not tie the two together

---

54   Calvin, *John Vol. 2*, 116.
55   Calvin, *2 Corinthians, Timothy, Titus and Philemon*, 57.
56   Ibid., 42.

irrevocably.'[57] He insisted that the Spirit can work in men's hearts apart from the Word and that the Word can be preached 'in a manner that is bereft of the Spirit.' In view of what we have already seen, this seems to be a surprising observation. In what follows we shall review in general what Calvin taught concerning the relationship between the Word and Spirit in preaching and then focus upon the particular points that Strivens raises. This will require an examination of the twofold efficacy of the Word and the relationship between efficacy and the preacher.

Calvin repeatedly insisted that Word and Spirit are joined in the believer's experience. Commenting on the Lord's promise that his Word and Spirit will not depart from his people in Isaiah 59:21, Calvin writes:

> Finally, he foretells that the Lord will never forsake his people, but will always be present with them by 'his Spirit' and by 'the word.' The 'Spirit' is joined with the word, because, without the efficacy of the Spirit, the preaching of the Gospel would avail nothing, but would remain unfruitful. In like manner, 'the word' must not be separated from 'the Spirit,' as fanatics imagine, who, despising the word, glory in the name of the Spirit, and swell with vain confidence in their own imaginations. It is the spirit of Satan that is separated from the word, to which the Spirit of God is continually joined.[58]

Several observation are appropriate. Firstly, Calvin reads Isaiah 59:21 as a promise that God will always be present with his people by both his Word and Spirit. He will always assist his church and will never 'allow it to be deprived of doctrine.' When believers are discouraged by adversity they should look to this promise and see that it assures them that they will always be 'supported and upheld by the word and the Spirit of which the Lord declares that we shall never be left destitute.'[59] Far from

---

57   Strivens, 'Preaching,' 65.
58   Calvin, *Isaiah Vol. 4*, 271.
59   Ibid., 272.

indicating that the church is sometimes left with preaching bereft of the Spirit, in Calvin's thinking, this verse promises just the opposite.

Secondly, Calvin understands the verse to teach that the Spirit will always be joined to the Word. Notice that Calvin uses the language of joining. While he is clear that Word and Spirit must be distinguished (they are not the same),[60] he insists that they are inseparable. As we have seen, Calvin considered the preaching of the Word to be of 'little use' and of 'no importance' apart from the efficacy of the Spirit. Therefore, since the preached Word always achieves its purpose, it must be joined to the Spirit. As Calvin observed one page earlier, since doctrine is 'never separated from its effect,'[61] nor can God's Word be separated from the Spirit. The possibility that God's Word would operate apart from the Spirit is always posited as a hypothetical, never as an actualised reality.

Thirdly, the Word must not be separated from the Spirit. This was the error that the radical Reformers had fallen into. Calvin condemned them for confusing the Spirit of God with the spirit of Satan, since it is only the latter that is separated from the Word. As Wallace comments: 'There is no more dubious and dangerous practice, according to Calvin, than to try to make contact with the Spirit of God by turning to any other source than the Word of God.'[62] ·

For Calvin, the stakes in this debate could not be higher. Strivens suggests that, according to Calvin, 'God is able to work in men's hearts by his Spirit apart from the Word, and the Word

---

60   This is arguably a serious flaw in Woodhouse's understanding of the relationship (John Woodhouse, 'The Preacher and the Living Word,' in *When God's Voice Is Heard: Essays on Preaching*, ed. C. Green and David Jackman [Leicester: IVP, 1995], 54–59).

61   Calvin, *Isaiah Vol. 4*, 270.

62   Wallace, *Word and Sacrament*, 129. See also: Walters, *The Sovereign Spirit*, 189–191.

can be preached in a manner that is bereft of the Spirit.'[63] From what we have seen we would expect Calvin to reply that the former comes close to the error of the radical Reformers and the latter fails to acknowledge the clear promises that God has made concerning the efficacy of his Word.

The close connection between Word and Spirit is also emphasised in Calvin's commentary on Psalm 119. He affirms that efficacy resides in the Spirit, but insists that this should not lead us to 'contemn the external word' since 'our illumination is to enable us to discern the light of life, that God manifests by his word.'[64] Later, when commenting on verse 133, Calvin turns to criticise the radical Reformers again accusing them of setting the Word at nought. They had failed to see that God has 'connected the external doctrine with the inward grace of the Holy Spirit.'[65] Word and Spirit are inseparable and no one should look for revelation outside of the written Word.

In Calvin's commentary on Ezekiel 2:2, he addresses the relationship between Word and Spirit again. Having noted that the efficacy of the Word resides in the Spirit, Calvin insists that 'the work of the Spirit is joined with the Word of God.'[66] He is quick to anticipate the objection that, since the Word is not effective in itself, it must be superfluous. He replies:

> [A]lthough God always works in human hearts through the Spirit, the Word is not without benefit. God gives us light through the sun; nevertheless, he alone is the 'Father of lights,' and the splendour of the sun is of no use except insofar as God uses it as his instrument. The same ought to be maintained about the Word, because the Holy Spirit penetrates our hearts and illumines our minds. All power of acting resides with the Spirit, and therefore absolutely all praise ought to be offered to God.'[67]

63   Strivens, 'Preaching,' 65.
64   Calvin, *Psalms Vol. 4*, 413.
65   Calvin, *Psalms Vol. 5*, 14.
66   Calvin, *Ezekiel 1–12*, 59.
67   Ibid.

The Word benefits believers because it is God's chosen instrument for transforming lives. The fact that the power resides in the Spirit does not render the Word nugatory any more than the fact that God is light renders the sun nugatory. Moreover, because God has assigned efficacy to the Word he has also conjoined his Spirit with it. Calvin writes: 'we maintain that when God speaks, the efficacy of his Spirit is added at the same time, for otherwise the Word would be fruitless. Nevertheless, the Word does not lack effectiveness, because the instrument must be joined with the author of the action.'[68] This is absolutely crucial. Because God's Word is efficacious for the purpose for which it was spoken, God has pledged to join his Spirit to it. While Stuart Olyott struggles to accommodate divine monergism with the use of means in regeneration, Calvin has no such difficulty.[69] He is quite happy to admit that the Word is the instrumental cause while the Spirit is the efficient cause. As Sinclair Ferguson has shown, this is thoroughly biblical;[70] Word and Spirit belong together.

Turning to Calvin's commentary on John 15:27, we see the distinct yet inseparable union of Word and Spirit emphasised again. Calvin criticises those who underplay human depravity such that they believe that faith can be formed by preaching alone and those who disdain preaching and claim secret revelations from the Spirit. Both have failed to see that 'Christ joins these two things together.'[71] The Word and the Spirit are *both* necessary for true faith.

Calvin's comments on Pentecost are also instructive, positing that the tongues of fire that came to rest on the apostles were a token of the efficacy of the Word that they preached. It assured them that 'power…would attend their preaching' and that their words would not 'simply sound in the air' but would pierce the

---

68   Ibid.
69   See Olyott, 'Where Luther Got It Wrong.'
70   See Ferguson's helpful discussion in: Ferguson, *Holy Spirit*, 125–126.
71   Calvin, *John Vol. 2*, 110.

minds of their hearers.[72] Moreover, this assurance was not given for
their words alone but rather, 'the Lord gave the Holy Spirit once
to His disciples in visible shape, that we may be assured that the
Church will never lack His invisible and hidden grace.'[73] In other
words, the gift of the Spirit at Pentecost assured ministers that
the Spirit would attend their preaching with power. This appears
to be very much at variance with Lloyd-Jones' claim that such
filling will be occasional and sporadic. There is no sense that the
Spirit will come and go or that preaching will be left 'bereft' of the
Spirit. Word and Spirit are distinct yet inseparable in preaching.
Likewise the Spirit worked on the road to Emmaus with the
express purpose that God's Word be understood. The Spirit did
not open the disciples' minds 'to see God's mysteries without
assistance, but to see them as they are found in the Scriptures.'[74]

   This same emphasis on the distinct yet inseparable relationship
between Word and Spirit is evident throughout the *Institutes*.
In addressing faith in Book III, Calvin writes that there is 'a
permanent relationship between faith and the Word.' Faith
is inseparable from the Word and it falls when it turns away
from the Word.[75] At this point, Calvin notes that he is not
addressing the question of whether human ministry of the Word
is necessary for the conception of human faith. He tackles that
question later in Book IV, a passage to which we shall return.
Rather, he wishes to emphasise that '[w]hether…God makes use
of man's help in this or works by his own power alone, he always
represents himself through his Word to those whom he wills to
draw to himself.'[76] This is a crucial text since it tells us that, even
when God works salvation without human means, he still does

---

72   Calvin, *Acts Vol. 1*, 51.
73   Ibid.
74   Calvin, *Harmony of the Gospels Vol. 3, James and Jude*, 245.
75   Calvin, *Institutes*, 3.2.6.
76   Ibid.

so through the means of his Word.[77] Even in the extraordinary regeneration of children dying in infancy God works *by his Word* in a miraculous fashion apart from human means.[78] Contrary to what Strivens has argued, Calvin considered it impossible for the Spirit to work in human hearts apart from the Word. The two are inseparable.

Turning to Book IV, we find Calvin insisting that God works in his people through the preaching of his Word *alone*. There is no suggestion that God will work in human hearts apart from his Word. All who spurn the spiritual food provided by the church 'deserve to perish in famine and hunger.' 'God breathes faith into us *only* by the instrument of his gospel.'[79] Moreover, although the power to save resides with God 'He displays and unfolds it in the preaching of the gospel [Rom. 1:16].'[80] The aversion to the use of means evidenced in Zwingli and contemporary writers is nowhere to be seen in Calvin. God works by his Spirit through the instrument of his Word. Calvin is clear that this has always been God's way of working. Just as he did not entrust the Old Testament saints to angels but raised up teachers for the people, 'so also today it is his will to teach us through human means.'[81] The authority of the Word is not diminished in any way by the baseness of the men God has called to preach it and although God's power is not bound to outward means 'he has nonetheless bound us to this ordinary manner of teaching.' In other words, humans are bound to the means that God has chosen to use even if God was not in the first place bound to use them. Those

---

77   This addresses the objection raised by Stuart Olyott that those who hold to 'mediate regeneration' cannot hold out any hope of salvation for those who are incapable of being outwardly called by the ministry of the Word ('News and Comment,' *Banner of Truth*, no. 557 [February 2010]: 7).

78   WCF 10.3.

79   Calvin, *Institutes*, 4.1.5 (emphasis added).

80   Ibid.

81   Ibid.

who, like the radical Reformers, refuse the use of means 'entangle themselves in many deadly snares' for 'the church is built up solely by outward preaching.'[82] Commenting on the *Institutes*, Forstman writes, 'since what is in [God's] word is sufficient, he never gives us instructions which can be added to his word. The Spirit is a teacher, but he only teaches us what is already in his word.'[83]

Calvin returns to the relationship between Word and Spirit in the following paragraph of chapter 1 of Book IV where he considers the meaning and limits of the ministry. He suggests that we should expressly note two categories of biblical text: firstly, those in which God joins the Spirit to preaching promising benefits from it; and secondly, those in which God separates himself from outward means emphasising divine monergism. We will return to this division of texts and Calvin's conclusions from it in our discussion of efficacy and the preacher, upon which it has much greater bearing. For now we need only note Calvin's conclusion; he writes: '[A]nyone who presents himself in a teachable spirit to the ministers ordained by God shall know by the result that with good reason this way of teaching was pleasing to God, and also that with good reason this yoke of moderation was imposed on believers.'[84] Word and Spirit are joined together and believers should approach the Word of God with the expectation of receiving what is pleasing to God.[85] As Calvin wrote in his reply to Sadolet: 'It is no less unreasonable to boast of the Spirit without the Word, than it would be absurd to bring forward the Word itself without the Spirit.'[86] In Calvin's writings, Word and Spirit are distinct yet inseparable. Alfred Lilley put it well

82   Ibid.

83   Forstman, *Word and Spirit*, 75–76.

84   Calvin, *Institutes*, 4.1.6.

85   See discussion in: Campbell, 'Word and Spirit,' 8–9.

86   Calvin's Reply to Sadolet, cited in: John Calvin, *Selelcted Works of John Calvin : Tracts and Letters*, ed. Jules Bonnet and Henry Beveridge, vol. 1 (Grand Rapids, MI: Baker Book House, 1983), 37.

when he claimed that 'it was the virtual identification of God's Spirit and God's Word as the sum of his relations with man that constituted the distinguishing originality of Calvin's teaching.'[87]

Given this clear pattern throughout his writing, it is right to ask what evidence there is for a contrary reading. Strivens cites four passages from Calvin's commentaries beginning with his commentary on 2 Corinthians 3:6, where the apostle contrasts the Law with the Gospel. Calvin notes that the contrast is not absolute but comparative. While the nature of the Law is to teach men literally so as not to penetrate their hearts and minds, the nature of the Gospel is to teach men spiritually. This contrast is not absolute, however, since grace was at work under the Law and 'even the Gospel is not always Spirit.'[88] Rather God has simply chosen to 'manifest the efficacy of the Spirit more in the Gospel than in the Law.'[89] Calvin continues in a passage quoted by Strivens:

> But when Paul calls himself a minister of the Spirit, he does not mean that the grace and power of the Holy Spirit are so bound to his preaching that he could, whenever he wished, breathe out the Spirit along with the words that he spoke…And so we are ministers of the Spirit not because we hold Him bound or captive and not because at our own whim we can confer His grace upon all or upon whom we please, but because through us Christ enlightens men's minds, renews their hearts and wholly regenerates them.[90]

Strivens concludes: 'For Calvin, then, in contrast with Luther, Spirit and Word are not indissolubly linked. While they normally work together and in tandem, God is not obliged so to

---

87 Alfred Leslie Lilley, *Religion and Revelation : A Study of Some Moments in the Effort of Christian Theology to Define Their Relations* (London: S.P.C.K., 1932), 85.

88 Calvin, *2 Corinthians, Timothy Titus and Philemon*, 42.

89 Ibid.

90 Cited by Strivens at: Strivens, 'Preaching,' 64.

do.'[91] It seems that Strivens' comments go beyond what the text of Calvin's commentary requires. Calvin does not address the question of whether the Spirit and the preaching of the Word are linked in a generic, absolute sense. His focus is much narrower and is explicated in the sentences omitted from the quotation. After 'words that he spoke,' Calvin continues: 'He simply means that Christ has blessed his ministry with His Spirit and so has fulfilled what was prophesied of the Gospel. That Christ should grant his power to a man's teaching is quite a different thing from that man's teaching prevailing in its own strength alone.'[92]

Calvin's concern was twofold. Firstly, it should never be thought that the *saving* work of the Spirit will necessarily accompany the preached Word. While there should be an expectation that God will use Gospel preaching to save its hearers (God is pleased after all 'to manifest the efficacy of the Spirit more in the Gospel than in the Law') there is no assurance that this will necessarily be so in any particular case. When Calvin discusses the relationship between the grace and power of the Spirit and the preached Word, he has in view the saving power of the Spirit, his *gracious* power. It is this that is not necessarily bound to the preaching of the Word – not the Spirit in a generic sense. Elsewhere Calvin insists that the Spirit may accompany the Word in judgment (see below), and Calvin is certainly not making any general statement about whether the Spirit accompanies the preached Word in this broader sense. He is simply insisting that the preached Word does not always save.

Secondly, and connected to the first observation, Calvin is primarily concerned that the reader should not attribute the

---

91   Ibid., 64. Gwyn Walters makes similar comments about the significance of this passage which should be rejected for the same reasons: Walters, *The Sovereign Spirit*, 161.

92   Calvin, *2 Corinthians, Timothy, Titus and Philemon*, 43. Walters also fails to give due consideration to the narrower focus of Calvin's words (Walters, *The Sovereign Spirit*, 161).

work of God to the preacher in any ultimate sense. He is tackling what it means for Paul to designate himself 'a minister of the Spirit' and he wants to show that the power still emanates from God even though it is manifested through the outward means of preaching. The minister's preaching is not efficacious because of its own strength. Rather it is the power of God. Nevertheless, despite this important distinction which is developed in Calvin's insistence that the Spirit is not bound or captive to minsters, Calvin goes on to insist that there does exist a 'bond and conjunction between Christ's grace and man's work.' So close is this bond that the 'minister is often given credit for what belongs to God alone.'[93] Far from separating the work of the Spirit and the work of preaching, Calvin insists that there is a 'bond and conjunction.' This is based on the gospel dispensation itself which consists 'both of the secret power of Christ and the external work of man.'[94] Once again we see Calvin affirming that God sovereignly works through external means. He is happy to affirm that the preached word is the instrumental cause of salvation while the Spirit's work is the efficient cause. Calvin distinguishes the saving work of the Spirit from the preached Word of the minister but he does not separate them. The Word and Spirit remain joined.

In summary, Calvin's concern in his commentary on 2 Corinthians 3:6 is twofold. Firstly, he wishes to show that the saving work of the Spirit does not inevitably accompany the preached Word. Secondly, he insists that when it does, the preached Word remains the secondary and instrumental cause of salvation. At no point does Calvin divide Word and Spirit or claim that they are not 'indissolubly linked' or operationally 'tandem.' Strivens is led to this conclusion because he does not distinguish between the concepts of distinction and separation

---

93 Calvin, *2 Corinthians, Timothy, Titus and Philemon*, 43.
94 Ibid.

and assumes that because the preached Word and the Spirit are distinguished they must also be separated. This is not the case.

The second text that Strivens refers to is Calvin's commentary on Isaiah 35:4. Calvin writes that God imparts transforming power to the Word 'not always indeed or indiscriminately, but where it pleases God by the secret power of his Spirit to work in this manner.'[95] Again, it is the saving power of the Spirit that Calvin has in view not the presence of the Spirit per se. It is the Spirit's power to strike ears and 'inwardly move our hearts' that is not always or indiscriminately given. This is unremarkable since it is axiomatic that the Word does not *always* save. Recognising this is quite different to separating Word and Spirit since Calvin considered the Spirit to be always present with the Word whether in judgment or in blessing.

Before proceeding to consider two further texts, we do well to note an additional aspect of Calvin's commentary on Isaiah 35:4. In his commentary on the verse, Calvin unambiguously recognises that the Word is the instrumental means of regeneration and sanctification. He describes it as 'a powerful instrument' for 'invigorating the feeble hands and strengthening the tottering knees.'[96] The work of striking ears and piercing hearts is directly attributed to the Word. The Lord 'assigns this office to the word.'[97] The Word is God's instrumental means for this work but this is not to discount the crucial and inseparable role of the Spirit. In the same sentence, Calvin recognises that God performs this work by 'the secret power of his Spirit.' For Calvin, in the one act, the Spirit and the Word work distinctly yet inseparably; the Spirit as the efficient cause and the Word as the instrumental cause.

Next Strivens refers to Calvin's treatment of Jesus' encounter with the Syrophonician woman to argue that Calvin recognised

---

95 Calvin, *Isaiah Vol. 3*, 65.
96 Ibid., 64.
97 Ibid.

that God sometimes works by the Spirit without the Word.[98] Upon closer examination, however, it seems that Calvin was purporting to teach the opposite and was simply seeking to demonstrate how Matthew 15:23 was not irreconcilable with this view. Strivens begins by rightly noting that Calvin expresses surprise that the Syrophonician woman persists in faith without a word from Christ. At face value, Calvin writes, 'this seems to be contrary to the nature of faith and prayer as Paul describes it in Rom 10.14.'[99] He continues, in a passage quoted by Strivens, 'although [Christ] then suppressed His words, He spoke inwardly to the woman's mind and so this secret instinct stood in place of the external preaching.'[100] This, Strivens suggests, is a statement we would not expect to find on the lips of Luther given his concerns about conceding ground to the Enthusiasts.

Several comments are apropos. Firstly, the context of the passage suggests the opposite interpretation to the one that Strivens' gives to it. Commenting on Matthew 15:22, Calvin recognises that the Syrophonician woman was from outside of God's people and would therefore not have directly received God's Word. Nevertheless he insists that she must have 'received a certain taste of godliness,' since 'without some knowledge of the promises she could not have called Christ the Son of David.'[101] Calvin opines that such knowledge must have come from the spread of God's promises into Gentile lands. The woman did not rashly invent a faith for herself, but 'conceived one from the Law and the prophets.'[102] In other words, her faith was not an example of the Spirit working without the Word, but rather of the Spirit working through stimulating prior knowledge of

---

98   Strivens, 'Preaching,' 65.
99   Calvin, *Harmony of the Gospels Vol. 2*, 168.
100   Ibid., 168. Cited by Strivens at: 'Preaching,' 65.
101   Calvin, *Harmony of the Gospels Vol. 2*, 167.
102   Ibid.

the Word (something that Luther also acknowledged).[103] This interpretation is confirmed by the text that immediately follows the sentence cited by Strivens:

> [S]ince her prayer was born of the hearing of faith, although Christ did not reply at once, yet there was always sounding in her ears the teaching which she had once learnt, that Christ came as the Redeemer. Thus the Lord often addresses His believers and at the same time is silent; for they trust in the testimonies of Scripture and when they hear Him speaking they do not doubt that He will be favourable to them although He does not at once answer their desires and prayers and only seems to be pretending to hear them.[104]

Again, it is clear that the Word is the instrumental cause of the woman's faith since Calvin immediately speaks of the 'tiny seed of doctrine…bear[ing] such rich fruit.' The woman's faith and prayer are attributed to the doctrine once received: the Word is the instrumental cause of the woman's response.

Secondly, Strivens' claim that the supposed difference between Calvin and Luther can be attributed to the latter's greater concern about conceding ground to the enthusiasts is not convincing. Calvin was just as concerned as Luther about conceding ground to those who would claim faith apart from the Word. Indeed, Calvin condemns Servetus for being 'absurd as well as ungodly' in misusing Jesus' encounter with the Syrophonician woman 'to strip faith of the promises.'[105] While the opponents might have been different, Calvin shared Luther's concern that faith could not exist apart from the Word.

Thirdly, it is surprising that Strivens should use this passage to argue that the Spirit does on occasion work without the Word since Calvin explicitly claims the contrary. In the passage immediately preceding the text, Calvin writes 'we must hold that

---

103   Luther, *LW 14*, 62.
104   Calvin, *Harmony of the Gospels Vol. 2*, 168.
105   Ibid., 167.

faith is always born of God's Word and takes its beginning from true elements, so that it may always be joined to a certain light of knowledge.'[106] Far from indicating that Word and Spirit are separate, Calvin's commentary insists that the Word is a necessary and inseparable instrumental cause by which the Spirit works.

The fourth passage which Strivens relies upon is a short section from Calvin's commentary on Amos 4:13: 'For behold, he who forms the mountains and creates the wind, and declares to man what is his thought.' Concerning the latter clause, Calvin writes:

> [W]e know also that the word of God is like a two-edged sword which penetrates into the bones and marrow, and distinguishes between thoughts and feelings, (Heb 4.12). God then thus draws men out of their recesses into the light; and he also convinces them without the word for we know how powerful are the secret movements of the Spirit.[107]

Strivens argues that this passage constitutes an explicit recognition that God works on occasion without the Word. The context, however, suggests a narrower reading. Calvin is discussing conviction of sin and notes that this is the end of teaching, 'that men may confess their guilt,' and a key function of the Word of God (Heb. 4:12). God is not, however, limited to using specific texts of Scripture to convict his people of sin. He also 'convinces,' that is convicts, '[men] without the word.'[108] Calvin is simply noting the secret movements (a better rendering of *instinctus* may be 'influences') of the Spirit in the conviction of sin. The Spirit may use specific texts of Scripture, he may not. This does not, however, mean that Word and Spirit are separate and it certainly does not suggest that God works in salvation apart from His Word.

---

106 Ibid.

107 John Calvin, *Commentaries on the Twelve Minor Prophets, Volume 2: Joel, Amos and Obadiah*, trans. John Owen (Edinburgh: Calvin Translation Society, 1846), 246–247.

108 Ibid., 247.

It simply acknowledges that the Spirit can convict of sin by direct appeal to our consciences; those consciences having already received God's Word either explicitly or implicitly (Rom. 2:15). Strivens is making a single passage do too much work.

One further text which ought to be considered as possibly lending support to Strivens' reading is Calvin's commentary on John 14:25–26. The verse reads: 'These things I have spoken to you while I am still with you. But the Helper, the Holy Spirit, whom the Father will send in my name, he will teach you all things and bring to your remembrance all that I have said to you.' Calvin notes that this is addressed to the disciples who might feel discouraged that the seed of doctrine sown in their hearts has remained hidden and smothered. They should not look elsewhere for revelation but instead be of 'good courage' until the Spirit, who is the inward teacher, comes to speak the same thing into their hearts. In the same way Christians should not be discouraged when they do not understand at once what Jesus teaches. Instead they should 'bring a ready teachableness' to the Word, listening hard and paying attention, and waiting 'until the Spirit makes plain what we seem to have often read or heard in vain.'[109]

Calvin recognises that the prophet Isaiah threatened unbelievers with the punishment of the Word of God becoming like a closed book, but opines that the Lord frequently humbles his own people in the same way. He continues:

> [W]hen Christ declares that it is the peculiar office of the Holy Spirit to teach the apostles what they had already learned from His own mouth, it follows that outward preaching will be useless and vain unless the teaching of the Spirit is added to it. So God has two ways of teaching. He sounds in our ears by the mouth of men; and He

---

109   Calvin, *John Vol. 2*, 88.

addresses us inwardly by His Spirit. These He does simultaneously or at different times, as He thinks fit.[110]

We have already seen that Calvin insisted that the efficacy of the Word resides wholly with the Holy Spirit.[111] It is therefore unsurprising to find him arguing that preaching is useless and vain unless the Spirit is added to it. What is surprising is his claim that the two ways of teaching (outwardly by the mouth of men and inwardly by the Spirit) are sometimes simultaneous and sometimes at different times. What is the significance of this statement? Does Calvin teach that the preaching of the Word is sometimes unaccompanied by the Spirit? Or does he suggest that the Spirit sometimes teaches apart from the Word? This passage is certainly difficult but, given the weight of evidence to the contrary in his other writings, we should answer both questions in the negative. Calvin's primary concern was to explain the different experiences of believers in listening to the Word of God taught. He was not making any absolute statement about the relationship between Word and Spirit in preaching. Rather, he was explaining that God is free to act by His Word and Spirit in different ways and at different times. He is free to act 'as He thinks fit.'[112] That Calvin did not intend to teach a separation of Word and Spirit is quite clear from the comments that follow. He turns to address those who would deny the sufficiency of Scripture and claim to have received some higher revelation from the Spirit. Here he groups together the Church in Rome, Muslims, Anabaptists and Libertines insisting that, 'the spirit which introduces any invention foreign to the Gospel is a deceiver and not of Christ; for Christ promises the Spirit who

---

110   Ibid.
111   Calvin, *Hebrews, 1 & 2 Peter*, 52; Calvin, *Isaiah Vol. 4*, 165.
112   Calvin, *John Vol. 2*, 88.

will confirm the teaching of the Gospel, as if he were signing it.'[113]
Word and Spirit are joined; they remain distinct and the Spirit's
workings may be experienced in different ways at different times
but they are also inseparable.

THE DOUBLE-EDGED SWORD

We have seen that Word and Spirit in preaching are inseparable
and that the Word is always joined with its effect. But we
have also seen that the Spirit does not always accompany the
Word in saving power and that the preached Word is often
met by unbelief. How are these statements to be reconciled?
For Calvin, the answer is found in the twofold efficacy of the
Word. The effectiveness of the Word is not dependent upon the
receptiveness of the hearer (although the nature of its effect may
be so determined),[114] because the power of the Word is 'in some
measure contained in itself.'[115] It is not an empty sound but is
rather 'something alive, and full of hidden power which leaves
nothing in man untouched.'[116] It is always effective even though
it is not equally efficacious for all.[117] For the elect it has the effect
of humbling and causing them to flee to the grace of Christ but
for unbelievers it simply hardens and judges their hearts.[118] Calvin
writes: '[A]s the word of God is efficacious for the salvation of
believers, so it is abundantly efficacious for condemning the
wicked.'[119] It is both a seal to the hearts of believers and a hot iron

---

113   Ibid., 88; See also Klaus Bockmuehl, 'Protestant Ethics: The Spirit and
the Word in Action,' *Evangelical Review of Theology* 12 (1988): 107–108.

114   See Wallace, *Word and Sacrament*, 91.

115   Calvin, *Hebrews, 1 & 2 Peter*, 51.

116   Ibid.

117   Ibid., 50.

118   Ibid., 50–51.

119   Calvin, *Isaiah Vol. 4*, 172.

to the conscience of the wicked causing their impiety to burn more strongly.[120]

This twofold efficacy is vividly brought out in Calvin's commentary on 2 Corinthians 2:15 where he recognises that the commendation given to the apostles applies equally to all ministers: 'wherever there is pure and unfeigned preaching of the Gospel, there this strong savour that Paul mentions here will be found.'[121] Ministers of the Word have this sweet savour before God whether their ministry has the effect of quickening souls to salvation or bringing death to unbelievers. This is because '[w]hether the outcome be life or death, [the Gospel] is never preached in vain.'[122] Commenting on the same verse in his Hebrews commentary, Calvin writes: 'Paul bears witness to this effect that from his preaching there comes a savour of death to the death of those who do not believe, and of life to the life of the faithful, so that God never speaks in vain without bringing some to salvation and thrusting others to destruction.'[123]

Calvin recognises that this raises the question of how the Gospel can be described as 'the ministry of life' when it brings death to so many, but replies that salvation is the Gospel's real purpose. It is only for unbelievers that it has become an occasion of condemnation and 'it is they who make it so.'[124] In a similar vein, he writes that the hardening of unbelievers 'does not arise out of the nature of the word, but is accidental, and must be ascribed exclusively to the depravity of man.'[125] When the outward voice of the preacher vanishes as though dead to the unbeliever,

120   Calvin, *Harmony of the Gospels Vol. 3, James and Jude*, 23.

121   Calvin, *2 Corinthians, Timothy, Titus and Philemon*, 34; See also: Calvin, *Harmony of the Gospels Vol. 1*, 295.

122   Calvin, *2 Corinthians, Timothy, Titus and Philemon*, 35.

123   Calvin, *Hebrews, 1 & 2 Peter*, 51.

124   Calvin, *2 Corinthians, Timothy, Titus and Philemon*, 35.

125   Calvin, *Isaiah Vol. 1*, 217.

the fault lies with the unbeliever, not the Word itself.[126] Whatever the effect it has in any particular situation, the Gospel remains the doctrine of life because 'it is the means of regeneration and freely offers reconciliation with God.'[127]

Calvin was quick to affirm that the sweet savour of the Word is in no way diminished by the fact that it is a savour of death to those who are perishing. Even if the Word were to do nothing other than condemn its hearers, 'it would be enough that it was a sweet savour to Himself.'[128] This is because even when it is met by unbelief, preaching either has the effect of convicting the ungodly and rendering them without excuse or of bringing them to repentance.[129] According to Calvin, preaching is 'not ineffectual when it renders the world without excuse.'[130] Therefore, although we should be 'deeply grieved' when people do not respond to the preached Word and indeed we 'ought to pray to God to give efficacy [unto salvation] to his word,' we should not be surprised at the twofold effect it produces. Instead, preachers should be satisfied simply with 'having the approbation of God,' in the knowledge that the Word is always effective either for blessing or judgment.[131]

We have seen that, for Calvin, the preached Word is always efficacious but 'it is not equally efficacious in everyone.'[132] Its efficacy is twofold: it functions either to save or to condemn. But, whichever function it fulfils, the preached Word is effective and represents a sweet savour to the Lord. Since the Word's efficacy resides in the Spirit, it is clear that the Spirit must always accompany the Word when it is preached. Sometimes the Spirit

---

126   Calvin, *Harmony of the Gospels Vol. 3, James and Jude*, 246.
127   Calvin, *2 Corinthians, Timothy, Titus and Philemon*, 45.
128   Calvin, *Pentateuch Vol. 4*, 328–329.
129   Ibid., 328. See also: Calvin, *Psalms Vol. 5*, 316.
130   Calvin, *Isaiah Vol. 1*, 216.
131   Ibid., 215 and 381.
132   Calvin, *Hebrews, 1 & 2 Peter*, 50.

accompanies the Word in blessing and sometimes in judgment. But it is always present. Calvin recognises exactly this in his commentary on John 16:8:

> For the Spirit convicts men in the preaching of the Gospel in two ways. Some are touched seriously and humble themselves of their own accord and assent willingly to the judgment which condemns them. Others, although they are convinced of guilt and cannot escape, do not yield in sincerity or submit themselves to the authority and control of the Holy Spirit; on the contrary, when they are subdued they groan inwardly and, although confounded, still do not cease to cherish an inward obstinacy.[133]

Just as the Word's effect is twofold so is the Spirit's effect, which is unsurprising given that the source of the Word's efficacy is the Spirit. Calvin's writings provide no support for the view advanced by Strivens that the Word may be preached in a manner bereft of the Spirit. It is certainly true that the Word may be preached without bearing saving results (although it should be noted that Calvin nowhere ties this to the 'manner' of preaching) but this does not mean that the Word is ever unaccompanied by the Spirit. Word and Spirit are distinct yet inseparable with the Spirit always accompanying the Word either in blessing or judgment.

Before we consider the relationship between efficacy and the preacher it is appropriate to comment briefly upon what Calvin considered believers ought to expect as they sat under the preached Word. To understand this we need to grasp the significance of faith and its reciprocal relationship with the Word.[134] Calvin writes:

> [F]aith cannot be separated from the Word. On the other hand the Word separated from faith is ineffectual. It is not that the efficacy of the Word depends on us for even if the whole world were false, He who cannot lie would not cease to be true. It is that the Word

---

133   Calvin, *John Vol. 2*, 116.
134   Wallace, *Word and Sacrament*, 130.

brings its power to bear on us only when faith gives it entrance. It is the power of God unto salvation, but only to those who believe.[135]

Faith and the Word are 'inseparable companion[s].'[136] They can be no more separated than can 'the rays from the sun from which they come.'[137] Faith rests upon God's Word and arises from God's promise of grace in Christ.[138] But the Word can only exert its saving power when it is received by Spirit-wrought faith. Faith and the Word are distinct yet inseparable when the Word's saving efficacy is to be experienced.

This means that if one approaches the Word with true Spirit-wrought faith one should expect it to be efficacious for blessing. While Calvin admits that the Word may sometimes appear as a closed book to believers; even this is for the purpose of blessing. The Lord uses such occasions to humble his people and to cause them to 'wait patiently and calmly.'[139] The normative experience is that the Word will be efficacious for the blessing of believers regardless of the manner or style of the preaching. The power is contained in the Word which is 'full of hidden power' leaving 'nothing in man untouched.'[140] Moreover, the blessing of God's Word to believers is not intermittent or hard to find. Calvin writes: 'we do not need to seek far, or to make long circuits, as unbelievers do; for he exhibits himself to us in his word, that we, on our part may draw near to him.'[141] God is always present with

---

135   Calvin, *Hebrews, 1 & 2 Peter*, 46.

136   Calvin, *Institutes*, 3.2.6.

137   Ibid.

138   Ibid., 3.2.6 and 3.2.7. See also: Calvin, *Harmony of the Gospels Vol. 2*, 167.

139   Calvin, *John Vol. 2*, 88. See also: Calvin, *Harmony of the Gospels Vol. 2*, 168.

140   Calvin, *Hebrews, 1 & 2 Peter*, 51.

141   Calvin, *Isaiah Vol. 4*, 166.

his people by his Spirit and his Word.[142] His supply of grace is not intermittent but a 'perennial fountain that will never fail us.'[143] The Lord has promised that He will never allow the Church to be deprived of doctrine and that she shall never be left destitute.[144] Therefore believers should approach the Word with confidence knowing that it is God's purpose to work powerfully through it for their blessing.

POWER AND THE PREACHER

As we conclude our discussion of Calvin's doctrine, we need to return to an issue that has arisen several times so far: the relationship between efficacy and the preacher. In some ways this lies at the heart of the debate and it is here that the analogy with Calvin's teaching on the sacraments is most instructive. Calvin recognised that the efficacy of the ministry was a great controversy in his own day and warned that people were inclined to veer off in one of two directions.[145] Some so exaggerate the dignity of the ministry that they take away from God what rightly belongs to him. Others understate the role of ministers for fear of transferring to mortal men what rightly belongs to the Holy Spirit alone. In the *Institutes*, Calvin advised that the dispute could be resolved by observing two categories of biblical text together: '(1) the passages in which God as the author of preaching, joining his Spirit with it, promises benefits from it;[146] (2) the passages in which God, separating himself from outward

---

142   Ibid., 271.

143   John Calvin, *The Gospel According to John: Volume 1*, ed. David W. Torrance and Thomas F. Torrance, trans. T.H.L. Parker, Calvin's New Testament Commentaries (Grand Rapids, MI: Eerdmans, 1959), 93.

144   Calvin, *Isaiah Vol. 4*, 272.

145   Calvin, *Institutes*, 4.1.6.

146   Into this category Calvin placed Malachi 4:5–6; Luke 1:17; John 15:16; 1 Corinthians 2:4; 3:9ff; 4:15; 9:2; Galatians 3:2; and 1 Peter 1:23.

helps, claims for himself alone both the beginnings of faith and its entire course.[147'] While it is nothing short of sacrilege for a man to claim for himself the work of illuminating the mind and renewing the heart, it must at the same time be maintained that 'anyone who presents himself in a teachable spirit to the ministers ordained by God shall know by the result that with good reason this way of teaching was pleasing to God, and also that with good reason this yoke of moderation was imposed on believers.'[148] In other words, God has ordained the preaching of the Word to be his chosen instrument for blessing his people and so believers should approach the preached Word with confidence and expectation. Preachers are the means that God has chosen for blessing his people and the preached word is the instrumental cause of salvation and regeneration.

In this manner, ministers are analogous to the sacraments. Calvin notes this in his commentary on 1 Corinthians 3:7, a verse which emphasises divine efficacy. Calvin writes:

> [I]t is important to note that [Paul] is accustomed to speak of ministers, as of the sacraments in two ways. For sometimes he thinks of a minister as ordained by the Lord first of all for the regeneration of souls, thereafter for feeding them unto eternal life, for remitting sins, for renewing of the minds of men, for setting up the Kingdom of Christ and the destruction of Satan's. Accordingly, Paul assigns to the minister not only the duty of planting and watering, but also provides him with the power of the Holy Spirit so that his labour might not be unproductive...On the other hand he sometimes thinks of the minister as a servant, not a master; as an instrument, not the hand; finally as a man, not God. Accordingly he leaves nothing but his work, and indeed that is dead and useless, unless the Lord gives effective power to it by the Spirit.[149]

147   Calvin, *Institutes*, 4.1.6. Into this category, he put 1 Corinthians 3:7; 15:10; Galatians 2:8; Colossians 1:29; and 1 Thessalonians. 3:5.

148   Ibid.

149   Calvin, *1 Corinthians*, 70. Calvin again emphasises the connection between the ministry of the Word and the sacraments in his discussion of 1 Corinthians 13:12 (Ibid., 281).

We recall that in Calvin's teaching on the sacraments he emphasised the distinct yet inseparable relationship between the sacraments and the reality to which they point.[150] The reality is always
present and available with the sign. Unlike Zwingli, Calvin was
unconcerned about the use of means,[151] insisting that such means
do not detract from God's glory but are a crucial accommodation to our creaturely weakness.[152] Thus, while the sacraments are
not efficacious in and of themselves (Calvin rejected the Roman
doctrine of *ex opere operato*), the Lord has joined his Spirit to
them in such a way that they are never 'bare signs.'[153] The reality
is present and available with them to any who come with Spirit-
wrought faith, and their power is in no way diminished if they
are received by the unfaithful.

In the same way, God has attached his power to the words of
preachers so that the realities of regeneration, spiritual feeding,
remittance of sin and sanctification are available whenever the
Word is preached.[154] 'Christ puts forth His own power in the
ministry which He instituted in such a way that it is evident that
it was not instituted in vain.'[155] Christ is 'not separated from the
minister.'[156] But in the same way as the sacraments are nothing
in and of themselves, so too the ministry of the Word does not
contain power in itself apart from God. Christ does not transfer
his power to the minister in a way that subtracts or transfers
anything away from himself. Rather he has chosen to make his

---

150   Calvin, *1 Corinthians*, 203; Calvin, *Institutes*, 4.14.15; Calvin, 'Clear
Explanation,' 316.

151   Calvin, *Institutes*, 4.14.12.

152   Ibid., 4.14.12 and 4.14.17; Calvin, 'Geneva Catechism,' 131.

153   Calvin, *1 Corinthians*, 203, 245; Calvin, 'Short Treatise,' 147–148.

154   See also Calvin, *Genesis (Geneva)*, 97.

155   Calvin, *1 Corinthians*, 70.

156   Ibid., 70. When Calvin speaks of God separating himself from his
ministers in his commentary on Malachi 4:6, he means it in the sense of
distinguishing between them in relation to the source of efficacy (Calvin,
Zechariah and Malachi, 629–630).

power 'efficacious in the minister.'[157] Again, Calvin emphasises
the distinct yet inseparable relationship between the Spirit and
the preached Word. Christ 'is not separated from the minister'
Calvin insists, but due to the tendency of man to elevate himself,
'we must make a distinction to correct this fault.'[158] Thus, while
God the Father does not allow preaching to be unfruitful he
'desires its success to depend on His blessing alone, so that all
praise might remain His.'[159]

Later in the commentary, Calvin returns to the distinction
between the instrumental and efficient cause of conversion.[160]
The fact that preaching is the instrumental cause enables Paul
to speak of the Corinthians as his 'workmanship in the Lord'
(1 Cor. 9:1).[161] But since God is the efficient cause, whenever the
ministry of man is being compared with God, 'we must always
speak of the effectiveness of the ministry in such a way that all
the praise for the work remains with God alone.'[162]

In summary, the efficacy of the preached Word resides in the
Spirit but this in no way detracts from the nature or power of the
Word. Just as with the sacraments, the Word is never empty or
spoken in vain.[163] It is always accompanied by the reality to which
it points. Even when it is not received with faith, the Word is
not deprived of its nature or power. For, 'we must not think that
God's graces can fail in themselves, even though their effect may
not reach us.'[164] The Gospel always remains fruitful, even if it

---

157   Calvin, *1 Corinthians*, 70. See also: Calvin, *Zechariah and Malachi*,
629–630; Calvin, *John Vol. 2*, 116.

158   Calvin, *1 Corinthians*, 70.

159   Ibid., 71. For similar concerns, see: Calvin, *2 Corinthians, Timothy,
Titus and Philemon*, 43.

160   See also: Calvin, *John Vol. 2*, 116; Calvin, *Hebrews, 1 & 2 Peter*, 255;
Calvin, *Harmony of the Gospels Vol. 3, James and Jude*, 272.

161   Calvin, *1 Corinthians*, 183–184.

162   Ibid., 183.

163   Calvin, *Hebrews, 1 & 2 Peter*, 51.

164   Calvin, *Harmony of the Gospels Vol. 2*, 71.

is just in 'power' rather than 'act.' It continues to operate as a means of grace even when it is not efficacious to its hearers due to the hardness of their hearts.

SUMMARY

We have seen that Calvin's understanding of the relationship between Word and Spirit in preaching is closely analogous to his understanding of the relationship between the sacramental signs and the realities to which they point. As a means of grace, neither are bare signs. They hold out the reality to which they point and that reality is *always* available to be received by Spirit-wrought faith. Far from separating Word and Spirit in preaching as Strivens and Olyott suggest, Calvin insisted that Word and Spirit are distinct but inseparable. The preached Word is never separated from the Spirit in that it retains its inherent nature and power regardless of how it is received. Moreover, the Spirit always accompanies the Word whether in judgment or blessing. This means that believers can approach the preached Word with hungry expectation knowing that it will be a source of blessing if received by faith. It is Christ's means of sustaining his Church and the Church will never be deprived of it.

CONCLUSION

In the introduction, we posed the question: is the Spirit of God present wherever and whenever the Word of God is preached? Should we eagerly expect and anticipate that the Spirit will accompany the preached Word or should we rather accept that the Spirit only sometimes accompanies it? Related to this, should we be seeking to cultivate methods in our sermon preparation (including prayer) and delivery which make it more likely that the Spirit will accompany our preaching?[1] In short, are Word and Spirit conjoined or are they separate in preaching?

We have sought to address that question from the perspective of historical theology in light of claims made in recently published articles.[2] The common theme of those articles was

---

1 Eveson, Strivens, Olyott and Hywel-Jones all suggest this with varying degrees of nuance, see: Eveson, 'Moore Theology,' 27–29; Strivens, 'Preaching,' 71–73; Olyott, 'Where Luther Got It Wrong,' 28–29; Jones, 'Preaching the Word,' 85–86.

2 There is much that could have been said about the topic from the perspectives of biblical and systematic theology and we explored some of these lines of thought in chapter one. Unfortunately, a more detailed examination of these points was beyond the scope of the book.

that there exists an unidentified body within contemporary evangelicalism which so emphasises the preaching of the Word that it has neglected the vital and independent role of the Holy Spirit. Word and Spirit have been conflated, these critics argue, and the power of the Spirit illegitimately transferred to the Word. Preachers operate on the fallacious assumption that the right exposition of the Word will inevitably bring with it the saving efficacy of the Spirit. Such a view, it is argued, has its roots in Lutheranism and can be traced back to Luther himself. There is an urgent need to return to the Reformed position (traceable back to Calvin) in which Word and Spirit are separated and an indissoluble link denied.

In the opening chapter we critically examined four articles that engage with the topic. We noted that there was a tendency amongst both the authors and those they criticise to fail to adequately distinguish between the concepts of distinction and separation. In John Woodhouse's emphasis upon the unity of Word and Spirit he comes perilously close to mixing the two and failing to observe their proper distinction.[3] Eveson, Strivens and Olyott, on the other hand, assume that distinction means separation and allow this to govern their thinking on the relationship.

In chapter two we evaluated the positions of the radical Reformers, Luther, Zwingli and Bullinger. We noted that a defining characteristic of the revolutionary spiritualists was their tendency to let the Spirit define the Word rather than the Word define the Spirit. They separated Word and Spirit in their thought and practice although the impact of this varied within the movement from the extremes of the Zwickau prophets to the more conservative approach of Karlstadt. Next we examined the teaching of Luther and considered whether there was evidence for a shift in his position following the events of 1521. We concluded that

3   See in particular: Woodhouse, 'The Preacher and the Living Word,' 54–59.

there was not and that, though tensions exist within his writing, there is no evidence that he illegitimately conflated Word and Spirit or transferred the power of the Spirit to the Word. In the midst of conflict with the radicals, Luther stressed the unity of Word and Spirit and maintained that the Spirit has bound himself to the outward means of the Word. This was important for Luther not only in opposing the radicals' claims to supplementary revelation but also in defending divine monergism. Despite this emphasis upon unity, Luther never denied the freedom of the Spirit or the fact that the Spirit is the efficient cause of regeneration. In the final part of the chapter, we saw that Zwingli distinguished Word and Spirit to the point of separation in his writings. This was fuelled by a concern to emphasise the internal perspicuity of Scripture, the sovereign freedom of God and the illegitimacy of man-made traditions. Unfortunately this disjunction also undermined, in part, his high view of preaching and was not followed by his successor in Zurich, Heinrich Bullinger.

In the third chapter we shifted our focus to the sacraments, having recognised that there exists a close connection between one's view of sacramental efficacy and one's understanding of the relationship between Word and Spirit in preaching. We noted Zwingli's refusal to accept that the sacraments were a means of grace due to his concern to emphasise that the Spirit neither needs nor is bound to outward means. Calvin had no such concerns and was happy to affirm that God uses means and instruments to confirm our faith. He insisted that the sacraments were not bare signs and that the reality to which they point is always available with the sign to those who come with faith. For Calvin, the sacraments are always accompanied by the Spirit for blessing whenever they are received with faith. The sign and the reality are distinct but inseparable and believers can confidently approach the sacraments with the expectation of receiving Christ.

This distinct yet inseparable relationship between sign and reality provides the crucial framework for understanding

Calvin's teaching on the relationship between Word and Spirit in preaching – the topic of chapter four. For Calvin, the preached Word is always effective for the purpose for which it was given because God's Word is inseparable from his action. In our study of Calvin's teaching, we found no evidence for the view that the Spirit can work in men's hearts apart from the Word or that the Word can be preached in a manner that is bereft of the Spirit. Calvin even insisted on the unity of Word and Spirit in the exceptional cases where God works salvation apart from human means. Because God's Word never lacks effectiveness he adds the efficacy of his Spirit to the Word. The preached Word is Christ's means of sustaining his Church and the Church will never be deprived of it. Therefore believers can approach the preached Word with confidence knowing that God will work through it by his Spirit. That is not to say, however, that the Spirit will always accompany the Word for salvation. Calvin taught the twofold efficacy of the Word; the Spirit either accompanies the Word in blessing or in judgment. But even when the Spirit accompanies the Word in judgment, this does not undermine the power or the nature of the Word. This distinct yet inseparable relationship between Word and Spirit has several implications for how we approach the preached Word but, before we turn to those, it is necessary to comment briefly upon later Lutheran and Reformed developments.

We have seen that, contrary to what has been suggested elsewhere, Luther did not conflate Word and Spirit and Calvin did not separate them.[4] That noted, it is undeniable that later Lutheran and Reformed traditions did move in these directions as the passages cited by Strivens demonstrate. The picture is only confirmed when one compares the work of H. F. F. Schmid on

---

4 Perhaps the projection of these later developments back onto Luther and Calvin is an example of the 'priority of paradigms' danger that Quentin Skinner warned against.

the Lutheran side with that of Louis Berkhof on the Reformed.[5] The inevitable question arises: what factors contributed to this change? A detailed consideration of this is beyond the scope of this book but it seems likely that later developments in Reformed sacramental theology played a significant role.

While Calvin's doctrine of the sacraments received widespread acceptance in the sixteenth and early seventeenth centuries,[6] its popularity waned and it was emphatically rejected by Hodge, Dabney and Cunningham in the nineteenth.[7] They preferred a Zwinglian doctrine, emphasising a separation between sign and reality and exhibiting greater hostility to the use of means. It is interesting to compare their position with that of Herman Bavinck,[8] the nineteenth century Dutch Reformed theologian, who accepted a slightly modified version of Calvin's sacramental theology.[9] Bavinck also emphasised the unity of Word and Spirit in preaching, insisting that the 'power of the Word of God and specifically the gospel must, with the Lutherans, be maintained in all its fullness and richness of meaning.' He derided the popular dualisms between the internal and external, and the spiritual and the material, insisting that the Lutherans were right when they maintained that 'The Holy Spirit is always present with that word.'[10] But, in words echoing Calvin, he insisted that

5   H. F. F. Schmid, *The Doctrinal Theology of the Evangelical Lutheran Church*, trans. Charles A. Hay and Henry Jacobs, 5th ed. (Philadelphia, PA: United Lutheran Publication House, 1899), §51; Berkhof, *Systematic Theology*, 474–476.

6   For a fuller discussion, see: Herman Bavinck, *Holy Spirit, Church and New Creation*, vol. 4 of Reformed Dogmatics, ed. John Bolt, trans. John Vriend (Grand Rapids, MI: Baker Academic, 2004), 558–561.

7   See my discussion in: Cunnington, 'Calvin's Doctrine of the Lord's Supper'.

8   Hywel Jones could have explored the differences between Bavinck and Hodge more fully, see: Jones, 'Preaching the Word,' 80–81.

9   Bavinck, *Reformed Dogmatics Vol. 4*, 4:473–482, 567–581.

10   Ibid., 4:459.

the Word does not always have the same effect—its efficacy is twofold. Bavinck continues:

> [The] Holy Spirit is not an unconscious power but a person who is always present with that word, always sustains it and makes it active, though not always in the same manner. In accordance with the unsearchable good pleasure of God, he uses that word for bringing people to repentance but also for hardening; for the rising but also for the falling of many. He always works through the word but not always in the same way. And when he wants to work through it so that it leads to faith and repentance, he does not objectively have to add anything to the word.[11]

Such a position is entirely consistent with Calvin's and it provides further evidence of a direct link between one's sacramental theology and one's understanding of the relationship between Word and Spirit in preaching.

In closing, let us trace out some practical consequences of Calvin's position and respond to a couple of the practical concerns raised by Strivens, Olyott and Jones. Firstly, Jones suggested that a right understanding of Word and Spirit (which for him means emphasising their distinction) will result in a 'spoken style' approach to preaching. 'It is not cool communication but white-hot speech – no manuscript or auto-cue for the preacher and no hand-out or overhead projector for the congregant!!!'[12] Jones may well be right to criticise manuscripts and hand-outs but it is surely wrong to link this to a particular view of the relationship between Word and Spirit in preaching. Even on his own view, it assumes an extremely restrictive (and even capricious) role of the Spirit to suggest that the Spirit will be obstructed by the mere use of a hand-out.

Secondly and more significantly, Strivens and Olyott suggest that a failure to separate Word and Spirit will result in a lack

---

11   Ibid.
12   Jones, 'Preaching the Word,' 85.

of dependency upon God in prayer. While I certainly share the writers' concerns about the famine of prayer in the church and recognise my own need for repentance in this regard (as I suspect most readers will), it is far from obvious that the writers have rightly identified the cause. They seem to suggest that uncertainty about whether the Spirit will accompany the preached word will motivate persistent, pleading petition. Hodge makes exactly this point in *Systematic Theology*: 'If the Spirit were always in mystical, indissoluble union with the Word, giving it inherent divine power, there would be no propriety in praying for his influence as the Apostles did, and as the Church in all ages has ever done, and continues to do.'[13] But is this the model of prayer held out in the Scriptures—that we are motivated to pray out of uncertainty concerning what God will do? Is not the emphasis in precisely the opposite direction? Daniel's heartfelt prayer of Daniel 9 was fuelled by what he had come to learn from Jeremiah 25. Jesus' instruction to pray 'Your kingdom come' (Matt. 6:10) is founded upon the certainty that the Father's kingdom will indeed come. John's exclamation 'Amen. Come Lord Jesus!' (Rev. 22:10) is immediately preceded by Jesus's assurance that 'Surely I am coming soon'. Strivens and Olyott are right to lament the prayerlessness of both preachers and the church but they have identified the wrong cause. The church's prayerlessness is not the product of confusion concerning the relationship between Word and Spirit in preaching but is rather the consequence of our pride and failure to acknowledge the all-encompassing sovereignty of God.

Turning finally to a consideration of the implications of Calvin's position for the church and for preachers today; it is clear that the unity of Word and Spirit in preaching has profound implications. The preached Word is never separated from the Spirit and always retains its power and nature regardless of how it is received. Preachers are 'the aroma of Christ' whether that be

13 Hodge, *Systematic Theology*, III:482.

from death to death or life to life (2 Cor. 2:14–16). This is because the Word is always efficacious, achieving its purpose either in blessing or judgment. Consequently, preachers do not need to enter the pulpit anxious about whether God will accompany His Word. He will, and preachers must be confident of that. As William Still so memorably put it: 'I never preach now without believing that something will be done that will last for eternity.'[14] This confidence should excite preachers and drive them to their knees in prayer. Moreover it should give great assurance to Christians as they sit under the ministry of the Word. Such ministry is God's ordained means of sustaining His Church and it is a 'perennial fountain'. Therefore believers can be confident that, as they approach the Word with Spirit-wrought faith, it will be efficacious for their blessing.

---

14   William Still, *The Work of the Pastor* (Fearn: Christian Focus, 2010), 9.

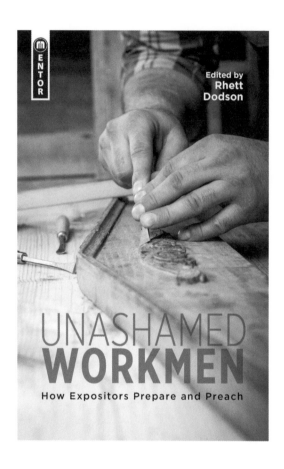

UNASHAMED
WORKMEN
How Expositors Prepare and Preach

Edited by
Rhett
Dodson

ISBN 978-1-78191-319-2

Unashamed Workmen

How Expositors Prepare and Preach

EDITED BY RHETT DODSON

Bringing together some of the finest preachers of our day, *Unashamed Workmen* focuses on the methods they use to prepare their sermons. You will find a variety of approaches and styles but they all share a passion for the Word of God to be explained and applied clearly.

Contributors: Peter Adam, Rhett Dodson, Iain Duguid, Ajith Fernando, David Jackman, Simon Manchester, David Meredith, Josh Moody, Douglas Sean O'Donnell and Richard D Phillips.

...a tour of the workshops of talented preachers, enabling us to look over the shoulders of these master craftsmen of proclaimed truth in order to learn how we might produce messages reflecting the beauty and utility of their sermons.

BRYAN CHAPELL,
Pastor, Grace Presbyterian Church, Peoria, Illinois

This is a great book. It brings together diverse and complementary voices from experienced expository preachers who are thoroughly committed to the Gospel. It is not a textbook. Its strength and freshness depend on the sweep of voices.

D. A. CARSON,
Trinity Evangelical Divinity School, Deerfield, Illinois

Unashamed Workmen is like looking into the mind and over the shoulder of ten master expositors as they prepare, and then sitting in the audience as they deliver the fruits of their labours.

HERSHAEL W. YORK,
Victor & Louise Lester Professor of Preaching,
The Southern Baptist Theological Seminary, Louisville, Kentucky

Practical and encouraging, this volume will undoubtedly further the development of faithful preachers and faithful preaching, all to the glory and praise of the Lord.

DAVID STRAIN,
Senior Minister, First Presbyterian Church, Jackson, Mississippi